Children Among Us

Foundations In Children's Ministries

Children Among Us

Foundations In Children's Ministries

Edited by Cassandra D. Williams
with a Foreword by Freda A. Gardner

Contributors

Elaine Barnett
Carolyn Brown
Rebecca L. Davis
Kathy L. Dawson
Mary Anne Fowlkes
Patricia Griggs
Sara Covin Juengst
Jean Floyd Love
Janet E. Thompson
Ross A. Thompson
Joyce MacKichan Walker
Carol A. Werheim

Witherspoon Press
Louisville, Kentucky

Office of Church Leader Support
Congregational Ministries Division, Presbyterian Church (U.S.A.)
Louisville, Kentucky

Book interior and cover design by Carol Eberhart Johnson
First edition
Published by Witherspoon Press
Louisville, Kentucky
Web site address: http://www.witherspoonpress.org
PRINTED IN THE UNITED STATES OF AMERICA
99 00 01 02 03 04 05 06 07 08—10 9 8 7 6 5 4 3 2 1

Library of Congress Cataloging-in-Publication Data

Children among us : foundations in children's ministries / edited by
   Cassandra D. Williams ; with a foreword by Freda Gardner.-- 1st ed.
      p.   cm.
   ISBN 1-57153-041-X
   1. Christian education of children. I. Williams, Cassandra D.
   BV1471.3.C48 2003
   268'.432--dc21

                                                       2003007145

Contents

Foreword

What if it's seven months to the next annual Christian educators' conference or even if it's next month, but you have no budget that will allow you to attend? What if you've heard of something that might be just what the Christian education program in your church needs to consider, but you don't know enough about it to make a case for it with your minister colleague or the Christian education committee?

Well, what if the people who speak and lead those workshops were as close as your planning calendar? What if the theory and practice of Christian education were explained by some of the best educators in the church in words that everyone could understand? As you sit in your office or at your table in the resource corner, wouldn't your heart sing and your mind race?

Here, in your hands, is food for the journey to which you have been called by God and the church, a call to be a church educator. Maybe you've already earned a degree or taken courses, read a lot or only recently said you'd give being church school superintendent or director of the youth program a try. This, then is for you. It is solid food in tempting, easily digested portions, prepared by those who are on the same journeys and know what is needed and what is possible.

- The Contents: the foundations and cutting edges of the teaching ministry of the church today.
- The Contributors: a who's who in Christian education today. Add your own name and join in the journey. If you are a pastor (in our tradition a teaching elder), or a director of Christian education, or a church school teacher, or a director of a nursery program or an after-school program, or have some other role in the educational life of your church, this book is for you.

Read. Gather with some others who, like you, are seeking to be both faithful and competent, and talk about what you've read and what it might mean for the purposes, shape, content, and leadership of educational ministry where you are. This is a book to be studied, chapter by chapter. It will be better understood if you talk about it with others who may have insights and illustrations that will help you to see how the information fits into what you are trying to do in your church or nursery, with young people in a confirmation class or a class for new members. And be proud to be a church educator, or consider whether it might be your call. Enjoy. And give thanks to God for such a valuable resource for you and those who share educational ministry with you.

—Freda A. Gardner

Introduction

The Office of Church Leader Support of the Presbyterian Church (U.S.A.) has produced this volume in partnership with Congregational Ministries Publishing of the PC(USA). Carl Horton, the coordinator for Church Leader Support, and I exchanged innumerable phone calls and e-mail messages and even managed one face-to-face meeting as we worked through the process of sorting manuscripts, setting parameters for content, and managing the logistics of publishing a multi-contributor resource. The generative vision for this work was of a single volume of foundational information for carrying out ministry with children. The outcome is a presentation of portions of an emerging picture of what it means to be equipped to execute faithful ministry with children. Early on, we changed the working title of this volume from *Foundations in Children's Ministry* to *Foundations in Children's Ministries*. This small change illustrates a significant truth—there is no single ministry with children, but, rather, a wide range of ministries that correspond to the multifaceted life of the church and the complexity of life as a child. No single volume nor series of volumes could embrace the fullness of that topic. *Children among Us: Foundations in Children's Ministries* presents what have emerged as essential components for outfitting those who seek to love and serve children in the name of Christ.

I count myself fortunate that in my role as editor, I have had the privilege of being the first to explore the abundance of information, passion, and compassion contained within these pages. The writers draw on a range of backgrounds and perspectives while they share exceptional expertise that is grounded in strong theoretical training and years of practical experience. Effort has been made to include that harmony of theory and practice within this resource. The reader will find expositions of solid educational, theological, and biblical principles complemented by practical suggestions, useable outlines, detailed examples, photocopiable charts, and comprehensive resource lists.

Although the writers worked independently and address distinct topics, certain themes repeat throughout the volume. When many independent voices raise similar issues, it is worth noting. These "compelling themes" may very well provide appropriate foci for the agenda of children's ministries for the twenty-first century. The commission to reflect on practices and traditions is inescapable within these pages, as is the directive for the entire church to support those who commit energy and hours to working with children. Each chapter reflects an awareness of our rapidly changing society, its impact on children, and consequences for designing programs. The importance of valuing children as children *in and of themselves* permeates these pages, and the inescapable truth of the formative nature of even the earliest days of life reverberates from chapter to chapter. This publication has been formed within—and will emerge into—a specific context, which is the ministries of the contemporary Christian church with children. As this is being written, the failings of the church in regard to children are making headlines and providing source material for late-night comedians. Jesus called the church to care for the "least of these." Because they are little, children are at extreme risk for neglect and abuse, and unfortunately, the church has often let them— and Jesus—down, not only by neglecting their care, but by perpetrating evil against them. The significance of relationships with adults and day-to-day life are underscored throughout this resource. Perhaps the most compelling theme of all is that because they are little, children merit our focus, our best efforts, our committee time, our budgeted funds, and our unconditional respect.

We are aware that there is more to be said in support of children's ministries than we present in this book. While providing us with invaluable insights and tools, the writers also point the way to other avenues of exploration, which may well be the mark of integrity for any resource: to share its treasures while illuminating territory yet to be explored. Ultimately, *Children among Us: Foundations in Children's Ministries* is presented in gratitude—for the God who calls each of us "child," for the church member who dedicates precious time and energy to precious little ones, and for children, who minister to us in their vulnerability and embodied grace.

—Cassandra D. Williams

CHAPTER ONE

Learning for the Mind and Heart: Education in Church School

Ross A. Thompson
Janet E. Thompson

The church school year has begun. The children have arrived in your classroom and as they take their seats, they are talking and laughing with each other. You recognize some of them because you have seen them at worship with their families. Others are entirely unfamiliar. As the room fills and the church school hour begins, the children begin to look up expectantly at you.

Now what?

If you are fortunate, you have anticipated this moment for the past several weeks. With the assistance of the church school director, you have chosen curriculum materials that will guide your teaching in the months to come. Perhaps you have also found time to decorate the room and the bulletin boards in ways that anticipate upcoming themes. You may also have a lesson plan prepared for today that you hope will fill the hour with activities the children find exciting and interesting.

Beyond the practical details of the first day of class and the days that follow, however, are broader questions that are less easily addressed. These questions are at the heart of children's educational ministries, but the demands of lesson planning and curricular development leave little time to reflect on them. They are questions like: What are children like as people of faith? What do children bring to the classroom in their ways of thinking about God and their questions about the world? How do children learn? What are the goals of children's educational ministries? Why do we have church school—and how should it differ from children's weekday education? How can we know whether church school makes a difference in children's lives?

How are children's experiences in church school to be connected with other aspects of their experience at church? How can teachers ensure that they have something to offer the children in their classes? How do we as teachers, nurture our own growth? These questions are at the heart of this chapter. They are questions that we writers have pondered as parents who have taught church school classes for many years. We have also considered these questions professionally—one of us as a university professor of human development and the other as an early childhood educator in a preschool program. Working with children of many ages, their parents, and teachers in church school programs, we have realized that these questions are central to reflection about the task of Christian education with children.

Our goal in writing this chapter is not to provide all the answers. We will suggest certain ways that children's educational ministries can be designed to serve children well. We will emphasize the importance of a developmental perspective, the significance of the relationships children share with their teachers, the necessity of active learning, and the value of recognizing the diverse ways in which young children understand. We will also frame questions that church school teachers and directors need to consider when designing programs. We believe that by considering these questions, even if the answers remain uncertain, all of us will approach our work with children more thoughtfully and with greater insight. In this spirit, this chapter is organized via a series of questions: What is the purpose of church school? How does faith develop? How do children learn? Why are relationships important to learning? How do teachers grow along with the children they teach?

What Is the Purpose of Church School?

For people who have grown up in the church, a children's education hour may seem as natural as corporate worship and as important as public education. It is an enduring, familiar, and expected feature of church life, but if we teach Christian education classes because we've always done it, we do not ask the essential question of the purpose of church school. Knowing *why* we do church school will guide *what* we do in church school. Additionally, as children's lives change in concert with fast-paced changes in family life and society, it is increasingly important for church educators to consider the relevance and role of Christian education programs for the twenty-first century.

What do children need that an educational program in church can provide? This question requires contemplating what children are like. What qualities do children bring to their experience of God and the life of faith? How can we assist children in their journeys of faith? The church has traditionally provided two distinct answers.

The predominant view can be drawn from the words of the apostle Paul: "When I was a child, I spoke like a child, I thought like a child, I reasoned like a child. When I became an adult, I put an end to childish ways" (1 Cor. 13:11). In this view, childhood is a period of preparation for adult capabilities and responsibilities. The ways that children think and reason will eventually be replaced by the more mature abilities of adulthood. Thus, one of the tasks of educators is to aid in this developmental process. With the assistance of teachers, children learn what they will need to know and grow in the skills that they will use throughout adult life. As they mature in faith, children will abandon earlier ways of thinking. This familiar portrayal of children is incorporated into our broader culture, where education is designed to help children grow in their knowledge and understanding and to turn childish ways of thinking into more mature forms.

A different view of children can be drawn from the words and actions of Jesus. On an occasion when his disciples sought to prevent people from bringing their offspring to him for a blessing—perhaps because they considered Jesus too busy and important to be concerned with young children—Jesus responded, "Let the little children come to me, and do not stop them, for it is to such as these that the kingdom of God belongs. Truly I tell you, whoever does not receive the kingdom of God as a little child will never enter it" (Luke 18:15–17). It is not clear what qualities of young children Jesus asked adults to emulate. Perhaps he had in mind their openness to experience, their willingness to trust, their lack of self-importance, their humility, or their capacities for wonder and amazement. It is clear from the attitude of Jesus that Christian growth involves the maintenance—not the abandonment—of certain childlike qualities. In some respects, this is unsurprising. Children have many characteristics that promote faith, including wonder about the world and life, acceptance of mysteries that are not fully comprehensible, belief in intangible realities, and an uncynical confidence in life's good purposes. If these qualities are lost with maturity, the faith experience will, in fact, become less genuine. Although many children lack the intellectual capabilities that enable advanced reflection and doctrinal comprehension, they are capable of a deeply intuitive realization of the divine. This is confirmed by those who have studied the faith experience of children and have noted that a child's earliest faith emerges from striving to make sense of everyday experiences.[1] For preschoolers, these experiences include wonder about how the world came into being and the need for security.

For grade-school children, questions about understanding oneself, about one's place in the world, and about good and evil generate reflection about God and divine purposes. For children of any age, faith is provoked and challenged by encounters with serious injury or illness, birth, death, parental divorce or remarriage, and social injustice. Faith is also nurtured by experiences at home, in the community, and at church school. Regardless of conceptual maturity or formal religious education, from these common and uncommon experiences children, like adults, interpret what happens to them as reflections of divine care and the world order.

The contrasting views of children as people of faith drawn from Paul and Jesus can be reconciled when we take into consideration that being a novice in *understanding* does not necessarily make children novices in *faith*. Although children need the guidance of adults to grow in their understandings, they bring to church school an awareness of God, questions about their experiences, an openness to belief, and other qualities that are an essential foundation to a life of faith. Faith and understanding grow and change with the development of conceptual skills, experience, and self-awareness, and in response to formal Christian education, but even young children arrive at church school with ingredients for faith that wise Christian educators will build on.

We propose, therefore, that a central purpose of church school is to *cultivate the development of children as people of faith*. This requires building on what children already know and believe, approaching children as developing people, offering catalysts to deepen understandings that are consistent with children's readiness to grow, and provoking hearts as well as minds. This overarching purpose is relevant whether the specific goals of a church school curriculum are to strengthen biblical literacy, enlist children in the practices of Christian service, devotion, and study, enhance understanding of the church, nurture a personal relationship with God, or simply to keep children and their families in the church. The purpose of church school is to facilitate growth in ways that build on the qualities of childhood and nurture understanding of divine care in developmentally appropriate ways.

How Does Faith Develop?

If it is essential for teachers to build on the developing capacities for faith and understanding that children bring to the classroom, then it is necessary to understand how faith develops. How can teachers anticipate and make the most of children's growing capacities? One way is to listen. It is easy for teachers to be so preoccupied with lesson plans that they fail to attend to what children bring with them to church school. When opportunities are provided for children to express their beliefs and feelings, it becomes clear that children's experiences of God are animated, vibrant, and personally meaningful. For preschoolers, who are likely to think of God as a superparent, God is real in the vividness of the natural world and in biblical stories of divine care. For older children, images of God are more complex and subtle. One ten-year-old, for example, described the immanence and transcendence of God in the following way:

> Well, God's inside of you in a way. In a way God's inside of you but in a way God isn't. He's inside of you because you believe—if you believe in him then he's inside you, but he's also all around.[2]

For children in difficult circumstances, the experience of God is tied to efforts to cope, as reflected in the words of another ten-year-old as she pondered her poverty-ridden life in a Brazilian *favela*.

> I shouldn't blame Jesus! I do, though, sometimes. He's right there—that statue keeps reminding me of him—and the next thing I know, I'm talking with him, and I'm either upset with him or I'm praying for him to tell me why the world is like it is.[3]

Those who have devoted considerable time to listening to children have found that faith development proceeds through several stages.[4] The earliest foundation of faith is established in infancy, when a baby's trust in the care of others provides an unconscious fund of security in the care of a divine parent. That trust also establishes a foundation for self-confidence for confronting life's challenges. If, however, care is lacking during infancy, the result may be a sense of insecurity in the divine parent and an uncertainty about personal ability to handle life.

The faith of a preschooler is magical, imaginative, intuitive, illogical, and filled with fantasy. Preschoolers are fascinated by stories of

the power of God and of the mysteries of birth, death, sickness, healing, miracles, and divine authority. Belief in the God who created
everything, can do anything, and is everywhere comes easily to a
young child who can perceive life in the inanimate world and identify purposes in natural events.

In the early school years, faith becomes refined by the stories that
children hear and tell about God and God's actions in the world. God
becomes anthropomorphized, represented in children's minds as a
superhuman figure who responds to people in terms of their faithfulness and fidelity, much as young children experience their own
relationships with human authority figures. This development
reflects children's developing appreciation for the importance of fair-
ness and reciprocity in human interaction, the significance of obedience to authority, and the belief that consequences follow one's
actions in the world.

Later in the elementary school years (and in early adolescence),
faith development incorporates religious teaching and the values of
the church, including the concepts of right and wrong and calling
and commitment. Older children perceive God as a personal, accepting companion who understands each person intimately. Thus, faith
begins to influence personal identity. The development of Christian
identity hinges on an emerging sense of self in the context of the
church and the wider world.

Faith is present in some form from the earliest moments of life,
yet faith also develops and continues to grow throughout adolescence and adulthood. As faith develops, later stages of understanding
do not replace earlier ones. Rather, the development of faith is like
the growth of a tree, with each stage building on earlier stages like
the concentric rings of the interior of the trunk. This is why we
adults retain elements of faith from earlier periods of our lives.
Which of us does not experience in prayer, for example, core beliefs
in God as a superparent despite our more sophisticated appreciation
of divine care? Which of us does not strive to perceive in the mysteries of life the prompting of God as a young child does?

Faith development intersects with the many other developmental
changes occurring in children's lives. Faith development builds on
growth in reasoning as children become progressively more capable
of thinking in sophisticated, abstract ways; it intersects with the
growth of self-understanding and identity as a child of God. Faith is
related to the development of conscience and moral understanding

as children consider the bases of right and wrong, and faith influences social development, particularly the relationships that children establish with peers within and outside the church. Faith development touches and is influenced by the multifaceted changes that occur in the lives of children. This means that how children respond to church school depends in part on other developmental processes in their lives. Wise church school teachers build on these changes in their efforts to nurture children's faith.

Since children come to church school at different stages of faith development, a variety of educational practices are needed. Children of different ages need different things from church school. For preschoolers who are captivated by the grandeur and mystery of God, teachers can use art, movement, song, fantasy, puppetry, and dramatic storytelling to explore God and capitalize on their intuitive wonder. Preschool is also an important time for children to begin to grasp the depth of God's care for them because of their need for security in a sometimes frightening world. For early grade-school children who understand relationship with God in light of important human relationships, discussing God through comparison with key persons can be especially instructive (for instance, How much do mothers love their children? Can God love us even more? Sometimes parents get impatient with us. Does God also?). Children of this age are also exploring their responsibilities to other people and to God. Simple lessons of calling, service, grace, and forgiveness are appropriate at this stage. For older grade-schoolers who are incorporating religious teaching into their faith, church school provides an opportunity to deepen their knowledge of church doctrine. This is why confirmation classes are typically taught at this stage. The growing appreciation of God as a divine companion who knows us and accepts us can open up new avenues to prayer, meditation, and reflection.

Understanding the interplay between faith development and other aspects of development can help teachers guard against offering lessons that children will misunderstand. Classic Bible stories like Daniel in the lion's den or Abraham's call to sacrifice Isaac can raise frightening questions for younger children who are not yet able to think abstractly. Many of the parables of Jesus will also be interpreted concretely. This is true regardless of what church school teachers *intend* for children to learn because children interpret stories through the prism of their own capacities for reasoning and understanding. Appreciating developmental stages will enable teachers to make the church school experience more meaningful and relevant for children. Understanding faith development can also aid in making other aspects of the church experience valuable for children—a topic addressed later in this chapter.

How Do Children Learn?

How do people learn? If you reflect on this question, you may remember the hours you spent in the classroom as a teen or young adult, perhaps trying to stay awake as a teacher droned on about topics that didn't really interest you. Many church school classrooms are patterned around the formal educational experiences that most adults have had. Consider, however, the last time you were motivated to master a new skill (feeding a baby, cleaning a carburetor, surfing the Web) or acquire a new understanding (about tax reform, your favorite sports team, or the latest controversies in your denomination). Your experience was probably quite different from the formal educational experience you recalled. As a *motivated* learner, you were enthusiastic about finding answers to questions that were personally meaningful, and you were committed to doing what was necessary to achieve understanding. You may not even have thought of what you were doing as *learning*, even though your knowledge grew and you were changed by the skill and understanding you acquired. Wouldn't it be great if the learning experiences of children in church school were like that? How might we make them so?

Recently, there has been a rapid expansion of scientific research about learning.[5] The implications of this research are neither complex nor technical, and many of its insights have long been intuitively understood by skilled teachers, but these discoveries can guide us in creating learning-friendly classrooms for children. Some of these insights are summarized and illustrated below with examples of church school activities drawn from our own experiences. You are invited to think of examples from your own experiences as you read.

Children are active learners. Although children have often been treated as receptacles of knowledge to be filled up with new information, the result has been that children can neither retain nor apply what they have learned. This is especially so when children cannot find personal meaning in what they are being taught. Children learn best when they can discover things for themselves through activities, discussion, questioning, and application. Treating children as active learners means that the goal of instruction is not just the accumulation of information, but understanding, application, and practical relevance. Where faith development is concerned, active learning is especially significant. Of what value is memorizing Bible verses without understanding and being able to apply them? Why should children learn the Lord's Prayer unless they can appreciate its significance for their own prayers?

Active learning occurs not when children are passively listening to a teacher, but when they are involved in creative thinking, questioning, and discussing what they learn. This requires give-and-take between teacher and students, opportunities for students to contribute, and a willingness on the part of the teacher to depart from the lesson plan to follow students' leads. Active learning also requires opportunity for children to apply what they have learned. After children have learned *what's so,* they need to be encouraged to consider *so what*—thinking about the practical relevance of what they have learned. Active learning allows children to formulate their own ideas and questions about what they have learned. This process reveals how well they understand new ideas and enables them to pursue questions about what they do not understand. In active learning, children contribute as extensively as do teachers because their learning depends on active engagement in the topic.

Active learning can make church school classrooms exciting and lively—and unpredictable. Here are some examples.

- One class of third-graders was studying the order of worship because the church was interested in children becoming more involved worship participants. At one point, the teacher suggested that the children create their own questions about worship. Although they were initially cautious, the students became excited about the task and came up with some keen questions such as: Where does the pastor get ideas for sermons? Why do we dress up for church? Why does the pastor wear a robe? Why are many parts of the sermon so hard to understand? The students composed a letter addressing their questions to the pastor, and they received a reply with detailed, thoughtful responses to their inquiries (the teacher thought that the pastor learned a lot from the children's questions about the sermons).
- A fourth-grade church school teacher wanted to enliven the gospel accounts of Jesus and his followers, so one morning the

children found that their classroom had been transformed into *The Jerusalem Post* newspaper room. Each child was given a press pass and a reporter's notebook. Over the next several weeks, children assumed the roles of investigative reporters. They used the gospel accounts and their imaginations to write stories describing how the events of Jesus' life might have looked to his contemporaries. The newspaper that resulted from their efforts was full of news accounts with headlines like "Disciples Adoring, Pharisees Mad, All of Jerusalem Is Confused," "Dr. Jesus Heals More People: 'Miracles' Amaze City's Doctors," and "Hydro-Walk Invented by Jesus;" newsmaker interviews with Simon Peter and Mary of Bethany; a cooking column ("Stretching a Tight Budget: Jesus Feeds 5,000"); weather reports ("Jesus Calms Storm"); Letters to the Editor; advertisements; and classified ads ("To Good Samaritan: Thanks. I'm feeling much better. A traveler."). The newspaper was circulated among the congregation, and the enthusiastic response pleased the children. At the congregation's request, a second edition of *The Jerusalem Post* was written to report the events of Easter, and, the following year, an issue of *The Bethlehem Journal* reported on Advent events. Through this interaction with the stories, the children came to a deeper understanding of the gospel accounts.

- Active learning is active in body as well as mind. It is inappropriate to expect kindergarten and primary-grade children to sit still for an hour or more, so a church school class designed for younger children will include everything from storytelling to singing, art, dancing, and group projects. One class of kindergartners used wood, fabric, and large appliance boxes to construct their own ark while learning the story of Noah. They then acted out the story for the class next door. As the children were building the ark, the teachers used questions and made comments to provoke thinking about what the experience might have been like for Noah's family. Children's minds were engaged and their understanding stretched while their bodies were busy.

Children are motivated to learn when new information is meaningful and relevant to them. Journalists know the power of a captivating question in creating a news story that interests readers (as they put it, 90 percent of a good story is asking the right question). Similarly, teachers are most successful when they can capture the interest of their students. Children are likely to be naturally interested in many of the topics considered in church school, but when they are not, it is wise for teachers to ask themselves why it is important for children to know about the topic. When that question is answered, teachers will be better prepared to arouse children's interest. Here are some examples of teachers' efforts to capture children's interest.

- One church school teacher hid quarters around the classroom before the children arrived and then invited them to find the coins. You've guessed it: the parable of the Lost Coin followed.
- Another teacher brought a large world map to class, and the students and their teacher devoted the hour to identifying the locations of Presbyterian mission projects. The teacher provided the students with lots of information about the countries and the people's needs.
- In one fourth-grade class, students were encouraged to rewrite the Lord's Prayer in their own words to help them better understand the language and to reflect on their own prayers.
- In another fourth-grade class, the teachers addressed their concerns about the children's lack of knowledge of their church and its history by creating a "church search" contest. Teams of children tried to discover the answers to questions about their church, (such as, What is at the top of the stained glass at the back of the sanctuary?). Some of the questions required that children turn to older members of the congregation, (such as, Where did a log cabin exist on church property?), providing opportunities for intergenerational sharing.

Children construct new understanding from prior knowledge. Everyone uses current understanding as a foundation for new learning, so it is essential for teachers to build on what their students already know. Generally, prior knowledge facilitates new understanding, but sometimes prior understanding impedes new learning. In a charming story called *Old Turtle*[6], inhabitants of the world disagree about what God is like. The stone describes God as a great rock that never moves. The fish portray God as a swimmer in the sea. The antelope sees God as a runner, and the island describes God as separate and apart. None of them can conceive God except through the prism of their own personal experience and knowledge. Children come to church school with a history of experiences that color how they think about their faith. Teachers are sometimes concerned about how little children know of the essentials of the Christian faith or the Presbyterian tradition, but exploration can reveal beliefs that shape how children interpret their experiences in church. One third-grade teacher was shocked to discover how children had misinterpreted the liturgical order of worship, with one boy perceiving the "prayer of illumination" as the "prayer of elimination." That discovery led to several weeks of study of the worship service, culminating in the children writing a liturgy that was included in the service the following week.

At times, church school teachers must build on understandings of faith that children have difficulty putting into words. One teacher noticed how often the children in a fifth-grade class seemed to think God was angry with them. The teacher suspected that the previous year's study of Old Testament stories in church school had contributed to this perception, so in upcoming lessons, the teacher incorporated activities to help the children understand God's care and forgiveness.

It is important for teachers to get a sense of children's current knowledge as a starting point for planning class activities. Sometimes this can be done through a series of activities at the beginning of the church school year (in one church, sixth-graders completed and then discussed a short questionnaire at the beginning of the year), but more commonly assessment precedes each new topic. Beginning each new topic by asking children what they know or think about it not only reveals children's understandings, but demonstrates the teacher's interest in what the children know and engages them in the activity of discovery.

Learning is a social activity. Although it is common to think of learning as an activity of individual minds, children often learn best when interacting with others. The relationships that children develop with their church school teachers motivate them to attend and participate in class and to develop interest in new topics. Additionally, it is no accident that education occurs with groups of students. Peers can be wonderful catalysts to new learning because, unlike teachers, they share common perspectives and experiences. Discussions with other students are animated because fellow students do not know all the answers and children can sharpen their own views by comparing them with those of their peers. Peer relationships also provide opportunities for children to understand the unique gifts of each member of the class; in so doing, they identify their own gifts and come to value the community of learning. Peers can also be valuable sources of support.

Wise teachers enlist peers in the learning process. In one confirmation class, students were divided into opposing sides and given a week to prepare to reenact the debate at the Council of Nicaea. Discussions can be stimulated among younger children about issues that do not require extensive preparation and about which children may have strong views (such as, what should the church do to help poor people in the community?).

The sociability of learning extends beyond the classroom to the family and the church. Family relationships can motivate new interests and learning. A church education program that connects with families enables parents to support children's faith development at home. Teachers must also be aware of what is happening in the church, the schools, and the community that touches the lives of students. The terrorist attacks on New York and Washington on September 11, 2001, meant that many children arrived at church school with frightening images and serious questions in their minds. Children benefit when teachers and parents are in close communication and coordinate the reflection that occurs at home and church.

Children have diverse learning styles. Good teaching incorporates different ways to learn. Through years of formal education, most adults have acquired the ability to learn by listening to lectures and reading a text. Some church school classes are patterned around this learning style. Most children can learn in many different ways, but children (like adults) differ in their *preferred* modes of learning. Some children learn and remember best through movement and touch, while others learn best through opportunities to represent their knowledge visually, as in a picture or a collage; others are strong auditory learners. Some children learn well through discussions in which they can share their understandings and listen to the views of others, whereas others learn best through stories of human experiences.

When teachers incorporate diverse modes of learning into classroom activities, they can reach more children. This requires some creativity! For example, we have observed church school teachers who have used incense to represent the presence of the Holy Spirit as some Eastern churches do (check for allergies and asthma before trying this); created simulations of a Middle Eastern home in biblical times that included samples of food; encouraged children to reenact

Bible stories and parables; and taken field trips to settings where the beauty of God's creation can be seen, touched, and smelled. In this technological age, there are software programs, videos, and films that provide additional avenues for learning. The goal is not to create a barrage of activities to stimulate every sensation, but to accommodate multiple learning styles and make it easier for more children to become engaged in new discovery. After all, faith is a matter not only of the mind, but of the whole being: It takes the breath away, quickens the pulse, and opens the eyes.

Learning occurs best when children can see how much they have achieved. How do teachers know when their lessons have had an impact? How can children know when they are successful in learning? In conventional classrooms, learning is evaluated through quizzes, tests, graded assignments, or sometimes in less formal ways. These assessments enable teachers and students to evaluate the learning that has occurred, and they reinforce the importance of learning.

In church school, of course, students do not pass or fail, but the end of the church school year may find both teachers and students feeling uncertain about what has been accomplished. It is important to find ways to assess what children are learning and to be able to offer them positive feedback on their efforts. There are many ways of observing the progress that children have made in church school. Comments and questions reflect understanding. Completed projects demonstrate mastery. Changes in behavior outside of the classroom and signs of deepening faith reveal application of knowledge. Some teachers make good use of occasional quizzes and game-style assessments. It is essential to remember, however, that memorization and "head knowledge" do not necessarily reflect growth in faith. When presented in an appropriate manner, assessments can give children the pleasure of seeing how much they have learned while enabling teachers to assess their educational efforts.

Contrary to many adults' experience of education, that of teachers talking and students passively listening, contemporary classrooms are animated, interactive, individualized, and less predictable. Taken seriously, characteristics of learning discussed above—that learning is active, that it is motivated by relevance, that it builds on prior knowledge, that it is a social activity, that there are different learning styles, and that it is enhanced by a sense of achievement— may lead to the development of learning environments that differ significantly from the traditional church school. The hope is that educational events will be ones that children enjoying attending, where learning is relevant and enduring, and where lives are changed.

An illustration of how Christian education might be restructured in light of our knowledge about learning comes from the Workshop Rotation™ model of Christian education.[7] This approach has attracted considerable attention nationwide because it uses developmentally appropriate learning activities in a format that gives teachers considerable resources and flexibility for adapting and individualizing curriculum materials. In Workshop Rotation™, each group of children rotates to a different classroom to learn about a topic through the creative activities of that workshop. For a four- or five-week period, each of the workshops focuses on the same story or theme, which means that children explore the same topic in a new way at each workshop over this period. Each teacher is assigned to a specific workshop and becomes a specialist in that activity, adapting it to the needs and interests of children of different ages. Many churches also enlist a group of pastoral teachers who move with a group of children from one workshop to another to provide continuity and nurture relationships. When the four or five weeks are over, another story or theme becomes the focus of activities in each workshop.

The themes of each rotation are similar to those used in a conventional church school curriculum. The parables of Jesus, the prophets, psalms, creation, Moses, and the Easter events are typical. The activities of the workshops, however, are atypical. They may include an art room, a drama stage, a puppet theater, a computer lab, a games workshop, and a music room. Workshops have also included a cooking room, a large room for movement and dance, a movie theater, and a geography center. Creative names seem to be the norm. We have seen workshop rooms labeled "Mary & Martha's Bed & Breakfast," "Eat Your Way through the Bible," "Sea of Imagination," and "Kingdom.com." Each workshop classroom is specialized in design and resources but flexible enough to adapt the workshop activity for children of different ages. For example, a stage might be used for simple skits for younger children and more detailed reenactments for older ones.

Workshop Rotation™ addresses many of the problems of conventional church school by reducing the demands of teacher training and preparation, preventing children who are absent from falling behind, and reducing the pace of the curriculum while enhancing its depth. This approach accommodates many of the learning principles described above. Children are engaged in active learning through opportunities to enact, discuss, play, dance, build, and think about different aspects of a topic. Various features of a given theme or story are presented in ways that address diverse learning styles. The likelihood of tapping into children's natural interests and prior knowledge, and thereby motivating learning, is increased as the material is presented in various ways. Most of the workshops incorporate the social aspects of learning as the children work interactively within their groups and the repetition of the theme or story allows children to build knowledge from workshop to workshop.

Why Are Relationships Important to Learning?

When adults are asked what they remember from their childhood church school experience, often one thing stands out—the relationships they had with their teachers. Long after specific lessons and activities are forgotten, relationships continue to have an impact. In the words of one blue-ribbon committee, relationships are the "active ingredients" of healthy growth and development.[8]

Why are relationships important? One reason is that they help to personalize learning. In the relationship established with each child, the teacher becomes familiar with the child's unique personality, background, interests, family experience, and learning style and is better able to individualize teaching. Although the curriculum material for the day will be consistent for the class, it can be connected to one child's special interests, another child's family background, or another child's preferred mode of expression such as drawing. Relationships enable teachers to become aware of events in a child's life that can color their church school experience, such as a family illness. Relationships can open up pathways for enlivening the class, such as discovering that a parent of a student has a special passion like storytelling.

Relationships between teacher and student also motivate learning. Check with any student—from preschool to college—and you will find that the response to the teacher shapes the response to the class material. To an astonishing extent, students are enticed to learn because of their relationships with their teachers. Topics that might otherwise be dry and boring become captivating because they are presented by a teacher with a strong relationship with the students.

Another way that relationships influence learning is more subtle. Shared activity provides a rich forum for implicit learning and growth. As teachers and children engage in activities together, children are affected by the examples of their teachers. A teacher's behavior speaks volumes that children are quick to hear and emulate. Church school teachers model faith for children through their words and actions. In one church, a teacher transformed the church's mission activities by eliciting children's contributions through simple projects, such as making posters to advertise a CROP walk or having a bake sale to raise funds for a soup kitchen. The teacher was also the chair of the church's Mission Outreach Committee. The children (and their parents) were quick to connect the church school projects with the teacher's broader work on behalf of needy people. As the children grew older, their interest in mission led to the beginning of collaborative outreach ventures sponsored by the church in other communities.

This view of the importance of relationships to learning differs from what we the writers refer to as a "traditional view" in which teaching is envisioned as telling students the information they need to know and measuring success by how well and for how long students retain that information. One problem with this traditional view is that it neglects children as active learners who require participation and give-and-take with the teacher. The relationship with the teacher is especially important because the nature of the teacher-student relationship can facilitate or impede children's sharing of their own thoughts and ideas. Additionally, as noted above, children enlist prior understanding in learning, and thus children of different ages will interpret information in different ways. For a preschooler, the story of Moses and the burning bush is likely to provoke concrete questions about the event (What did God's voice sound like? Was the bush like our family's gas fireplace at home?), whereas to a grade-schooler, the story may be a lesson about obedience, and for an older child, the bush can be conceived of as an abstract symbol of holiness. In a view of the teacher-student relationship that sees the teacher as the imparter of information, there tends to be one "correct" understanding of a story with little room for students' personal appropriation of its meaning. When learning is seen as an activity shared by teacher and student, the views of children as well as those of the adults are important. There is room for the unique perspectives that children bring to the learning process from their backgrounds, experiences, and stages of development. The teacher's task, then, is to provide the opportunities and catalysts for discovery.

As central as the relationship with the teacher is to the experience of children in church school, it is not the only important relationship. The relationships that children develop with other children are also significant. In fact, in a situation in which children annually "graduate" from one teacher to another, peers may provide the primary continuity in relationships in church school. Peers also provoke new understanding through discussions and disagreements. There is, therefore, considerable value to conducting group-building activities early in the church school year to enhance peer relationships.

Relationships *among* adults are also important for children's learning. Team-teaching[9] a church school class can provide teachers with the support they need to remain fresh and creative. Two or more teachers working together can brainstorm, share ideas about what works with the class, and divide responsibilities according to their strengths and preferences. An experienced teacher can be a guide to a novice teacher, and will feel less isolated as a result. One of the advantages of team-teaching is that teachers with different personalities will connect with different children in the class. Teachers will also benefit from collaboration with others in the Christian education program, especially those who provide leadership to the program, in their efforts. Formal gatherings such as in-service training events are great opportunities for classroom teachers to become better prepared, experience the support of other teachers, and enjoy the camaraderie of a teaching community, but informal hallway conversations, sharing snacks after class in the resource room, and exchanges about teaching challenges can accomplish the same purposes. The key is for teachers to feel that they are part of the church's larger educational community.

Good relationships build on other relationships. Strong partnerships among teachers and good communication between teachers and parents provide a foundation for the development of teacher-student relationships that promote learning and a supportive peer environment. It is not always easy to develop strong relationships with each of the children in a church school classroom: Some children present greater challenges than others and patience is required. It is important for church school teachers to view children through the filter of God's love and to remember that each child is the teacher's equal in the sense that he or she is created by God and provided redemption in Christ.

How Does Christian Education Relate to Children's Broader Experience in Church?

Children learn all the time, within the classroom and outside it. Much of their learning is nondeliberate, consisting of unconscious lessons obtained through experience and awareness. Children learn from the acceptance they feel, the respect their feelings and opinions receive, and the genuineness of adult warmth. One of the goals of Christian education is to ensure that church school classrooms, as well as lesson plans, are affirming and meaningful, that unspoken and spoken messages affirm that children are welcome.

It is equally important that children are welcomed beyond the classroom within the church community. This is a challenge that requires intentional efforts. Those who plan worship services and organize other church activities may do so with little sensitivity to the needs and capabilities of children as people of faith. This can be true even in churches that advocate intergenerational inclusiveness. Children may *attend* corporate worship but find that the words of the hymns, liturgy, or sermon are incomprehensible or, even worse, frightening. No one deliberately plans worship services to bore or alienate children. Rather, church activities tend to be organized with adult attendants in mind, thus failing the ideal of intergenerational inclusiveness.

It is wonderfully challenging to plan corporate worship and other church activities with sensitivity to the needs of both children and adults.[10] Because of their sensitivity to the needs of children as people of faith, church school educators may play a special role in ensuring that worship and other activities are inclusive of children. The effort to create friendly environments for children throughout the church community is consistent with the educator's awareness that children learn both inside and outside the classroom. What messages might children receive about their place in the church and the nature of worship when they experience opportunities to grow and learn at church school, but cannot understand the words of the worship services they are required to attend? Creating a welcoming environment for children throughout the church enhances the benefits of church school for children and demonstrates respect for children as people of faith.[11]

How Do Teachers Grow Along with the Children They Teach?

Teaching well is challenging. Teaching about things that matter can be very difficult. Church school teachers have to confront their own doubts and uncertainties when preparing for the class session. Children will struggle with many of the same things that adults do, such as the anger and judgment of God in some of the Old Testament stories and some of the difficult sayings attributed to Jesus in the Gospels. When taken seriously, teaching about faith confronts teachers with the challenges of their own faith development. In accepting the task of leading children toward a deeper understanding of the divine, teachers also must become learners.

The courage to teach[12] thus derives from an adult's willingness to sit alongside a child as a novice in faith. Although the adult has more knowledge and experience, he or she does not have all the answers to the challenging questions of living a life of faith in God. In order to teach well, teachers must learn and grow in their faith along with the children in their classrooms. Well-conceived church school programs reflect an appreciation that the learning opportunities that teachers provide for children arise from their own experiences of faith. Teachers, therefore, require others to provide them with support, to nurture their own awareness of God, and to help them toward greater understandings of faith. Those who support teachers in this way can be directors of Christian education programs, pastors, or other teachers. Support of teachers may require some creativity in programming. The conventional scheduling of children's church school classes to conflict with all adult education opportunities, for example, is one way of ensuring teacher burnout.

In addition to knowledge and experience, teachers need to bring to the church classroom an understanding of children as developing people, an awareness of the importance of active learning, a recognition of the significance of relationships for learning, and a commitment to reaching the hearts as well as the minds of students. The teacher is on the front lines, bringing to the classroom the support of the community of faith and the resources that come from being nurtured within that community. Children bring to the classroom their own special gifts and offer to their teachers an openness to experience, a guileless wonder about the world, an unhampered acceptance of incomprehensible mysteries, and an unblemished confidence in life's good purposes. These are characteristics that Jesus recognized as the cornerstones of mature faith. They also bring excitement to church classrooms. From this combination of what students and teachers bring to the classroom come learning and growth for both children and adults.

Notes

1. Robert Coles, *The Spiritual Life of Children* (Boston: Houghton Mifflin, 1990). James W. Fowler, *Stages of Faith* (New York: HarperCollins, 1981). Jonathan Kozol, *Amazing Grace* (New York: Crown, 1995).

2. Fowler, 139.

3. Coles, 91.

4. See especially Fowler.

5. *How People Learn,* Committee on Developments in the Science of Learning, National Research Council. (Washington, DC: National Academies Press, 2000).

6. Douglas Wood, *Old Turtle* (Duluth, MN: Pfeiffer-Hamilton, 1992).

7. The Workshop Rotation Model™ was developed by Neil MacQueen and Melissa Armstrong Hansche. For more information go to www.Rotation.org.

8. From *Neurons to Neighborhoods: The Science of Early Childhood Development,* Committee on Integrating, National Research Council (Washington, DC: National Academies Press, 2000).

9. Team teaching is not to be confused with teacher rotation, in which two or more teachers work in the classroom on a rotating schedule, with only one teacher present each week. Although teacher rotation can be attractive to volunteers because it reduces the responsibilities of teaching church school, it does not provide children with the benefits of consistent relationships with teachers because children see each teacher only a few times a month. Additionally, teacher rotation means that each class is taught by a teacher who probably was not present at the previous class session and will not be present during the following session to provide continuity in children's understanding. For these reasons, we believe that team teaching is far more beneficial for children and teachers than is teacher rotation.

10. David Ng and Virginia Thomas, *Children in the Worshiping Community* (Atlanta, GA: John Knox Press, 1981).

11. Ross A. Thompson and Brandy Randall, "A Standard of Living Adequate for Children's Spiritual Development," in *Implementing the UN Convention on the Rights of the Child: A Standard of Living Adequate for Development,* ed. Arlene B. Andrews and Natalie H. Kaufman. (Westport, CT: Praeger, 1999).

12. Parker J. Palmer, *The Courage to Teach: Exploring the Inner Landscape of a Teacher's Life* (San Francisco: Jossey-Bass, 1998).

CHAPTER TWO

When Does Faith Begin? Child Development in a Faith Perspective

Kathy L. Dawson

> An argument arose among them as to which one of them was the greatest. But Jesus, aware of their inner thoughts, took a little child and put it by his side, and said to them, "Whoever welcomes this child in my name welcomes me, and whoever welcomes me welcomes the one who sent me; for the least among all of you is the greatest (Luke 9:46–48).

You may have heard this biblical text since childhood, but have you ever wondered about the silent child in the scene? How old was the child that Jesus placed before the disciples? Was the child old enough to make a profession of faith? Was the child able to answer questions from the disciples about what it means to believe in God? Could the child stand or was he or she placed by Jesus for physical support? Our responses to questions such as these are indicative of our understandings of when faith begins and, consequently, have an impact on how we structure church programs for young children.

When does faith begin? This chapter begins with a look at evidence drawn from scripture and theories of human development to support the claim that *faith begins before a child is able to give verbal expression to it*. Part of the difficulty in addressing the question of when faith begins lies in the many definitions of faith that are in current use, so different understandings of faith will be considered in a section titled, "Receiving the Kingdom of God." Finally the implications of faith experience before the age of seven for children's programming are discussed in "Welcoming the Child." Young children often have little opportunity or ability to make their spiritual beliefs known to others. One of the purposes of this chapter is to provide tools for observing extant faith and nurturing growth in young children.

Jesus Put a *Little Child* by His Side

In the version of the story found in the Gospel according to Mark (9:36), after placing a little child among his disciples, Jesus takes the child in his arms. How old is this nameless, silent child? The Greek word, *paidion*, used in this passage normally refers to a child not yet seven.[1] In Luke's version of the story (18:15), *brephos,* which means infant or babe, is used.

Children are viewed within the discipline of developmental psychology in at least two ways with regard to their relationship to their environment. For purposes of this discussion, these approaches will be termed "classic developmentalist" and "cultural developmentalist." The classic developmentalists have influenced education in general, and Christian education in particular, for decades. Classic developmental theories come from two basic schools: structuralists, represented by persons like Jean Piaget and Lawrence Kohlberg; and psychoanalysts, represented by persons like Sigmund and Anna Freud, Erik Erikson, Donald W. Winnicott, and Ana-Maria Rizzuto. Some contemporary classic developmentalists, such as Robert Kegan and James Fowler, have tried to combine these two schools in their work. Classic developmental theories, though different in content, share several common understandings, including: 1. Development is universal—all children everywhere develop the same sequence of skills or thoughts. 2. There is no need for a special environment to attain stages. 3. Everyone must pass through these same stages or phases in the same order. 4. The transitions between stages have rules and processes that are important for future development.[2]

An emerging group of theorists, referred to here as "cultural developmentalists," rejects the first two understandings of the classic developmentalists identified above. Maria Montessori, Lev Vygotsky, David Feldman, and Howard Gardner represent the cultural developmentalist approach. These developmentalists emphasize the role that the cultural environment plays in shaping the skills, thoughts, and beliefs of the young child. While not contending that all things are culturally based, these theorists have underscored the importance of the value that a culture puts on a particular skill or belief as a contributing factor in its development within an individual. According to cultural developmentalists, these valued skills and beliefs are housed within domains such as music, science, art, athletics, and writing. As this discussion proceeds with a comparative look at younger children through the lenses of classic and cultural developmental thought, it will be helpful for readers to spend some time with infants and children or recall young children they have known.

Ages 0–2: Even Infants[3]

The newborn infant appears tiny and fragile to the adult observer. The child's head needs to be held because the neck is not yet strong enough to support it. The infant sleeps most of the time and makes his or her needs known through cries and increased muscle activity. Innate reflexes guide movements of grasping and sucking as the baby seeks to gratify life's most basic needs.[4] The dependent infant demands adult protection, but does the infant have faith? The answer to this question depends on how faith is defined. If faith is defined as the belief and trust in something that is beyond one's self or, as termed by some, "transcendence," then indeed we can say that the infant has faith. This proposal is supported by the various developmental theories.

Both classic and cultural developmentalists maintain that all children *develop* some concept of the self as separate from the objects surrounding them. A newborn infant views the mother's breast and face as an extension of his or her own body. There is no mom and I, there is only I. This is what Jean Piaget and others termed "egocentrism"—the appropriation of the world as an extension of the self. Part of the journey of development for the infant is moving away from this singular view of the self and the objects that surround it.

How does a child accomplish this task? Classic developmentalists have focused much of their time and energy on answering this question. Piaget first noticed that infants gradually move from being subject to innate reflexes to *having* reflexes and movements that are under their control.[5] An infant's early exploration of the limits of the self form what Piaget termed a "sensorimotor perspective." Sensorimotor means that infants and toddlers do their thinking by moving and sensing. As they begin to interact with their environment, infants learn to differentiate between the hand that is part of their own bodies and the hands that reach down to pick them up, hold them, and minister to their needs. Neo-Piagetian Robert Kegan depicts this period as follows.

When the child is able to have his reflexes rather than be them, he stops thinking he causes the world to go dark when he closes his eyes.[6]

Psychoanalysts have long been interested in this very early period of an infant's life. As early as in the writings of Sigmund Freud is found the suggestion that future relations and the emotions that surround them are grounded in the young child's ability to take an external object into its self or ego.[7] This process was later defined by Donald W. Winnicott, Margaret Mahler, and others of the Object Relations school of psychoanalysis as "differentiation and separation." According to Winnicott, as early as the fourth month of an infant's life, objects may become creative links between the child's self and mother.[8] These "transitional objects" may be physical items like a beloved stuffed animal or blanket, or they may be a favorite bedtime song or story.

As the infant's differentiation continues, play emerges as the child and the primary caregiver play at hiding and finding each other. Games such as peek-a-boo and hiding behind something seem to transcend cultural boundaries. As play and creativity continue and new objects are internalized, a self begins to emerge within the child. If the relationship with the primary caregiver (usually the mother) has been "good enough"[9]—that is, needs have been met and transitional space allowed for creative distancing—then the child's ability to work with various cultural and religious symbols is secured.[10] If not, a "false self" is likely to emerge wherein more emphasis is placed on meeting the needs of the caregiver at the expense of creativity and originality.[11] This has significant implications for church nurseries, which will be discussed later in this chapter.

In her book *The Birth of the Living God: A Psychoanalytical Study*, Ana-Maria Rizzuto offers the religious community insights into how this transitional space of play and creativity allows children to begin forming images of God as an amalgamation of the images of parents and other important caregivers in their environment. Even before the age of two years, children experience their images of God as they do all objects in their environment: through the use of their senses.[12] The hiding and finding games that play a role in differentiation also help children form a relationship with the God they cannot see. The first religious song that many children learn is "Jesus Loves Me." As the song states, we know that we are loved by Jesus because the Bible tells us so. Thus, the Bible may be seen as a transitional object that connects us to the Jesus we cannot see.

It is not enough, however, to simply connect with and separate from the objects and/or persons in our environment. An infant also learns to trust or mistrust these important relationships. Here the work of Erik Erikson, another psychoanalyst who has applied the work of Sigmund Freud to very young children, becomes important. In Erikson's system, the infant is working through a life crisis of sorts about whether or not to trust the objects and others in his or her environment.

> The first demonstration of social trust in the baby is the ease of his feeding, the depth of his sleep, the relaxation of his bowels.[13]

This trust is both internal and external. The baby relies on caregivers to be consistent and caring. The infant also begins to trust that his or her body can be controlled and is reliable. Part of what children are doing when they put objects in their mouths is determining whether or not the objects are trustworthy. It is a way of bringing the internal and external worlds into contact. If a child does not establish this basic trust in infancy, it can lead to the development of psychological difficulties and the need for therapy to establish trust later in life.[14]

Erikson pairs the attitude of trust in the infant with the attitude of faith in the parents. It is because the parents are faithful in their caring that the infant has the ability to trust. For Erikson, his attitude is institutionalized in religion, where the believer trusts in an infinite Parent/Provider who will be trustworthy in meeting physical and spiritual needs.[15] Trusting, therefore, is a relational enterprise. There is mutuality between parent and infant as the baby is nourished and changed, held and cooed over. Even before the infant can understand the language of the parent, a relaxation and surrendering occur that take great courage, hope, and faith.[16]

To establish trust, it is not enough simply to separate from the objects and persons in the infant's environment. There is also a growing capacity during this time to believe that the object or person remains constant even when not within the infant's grasp or sensing world. This move to "object constancy" is crucial in the life of faith, which depends on trust in the unseen Other.[17] If object constancy were not established, no one would ever volunteer for a church nursery again. Those who have worked with young children know the characteristics of those who have not yet come to trust that their parents still exist when they are not physically present. These are the children who cry the moment the parents leave the room and do not cease until the parents return. In terms of faith, if adults have not developed the capacity of object constancy, faith will be dependent on those times when God's presence is felt but will cease to exist when God seems far away.[18]

Usually between the ages of one and two, with the development of object constancy the child enters a new stage of development and of faith. The infant is busy becoming a toddler by learning the skills of sitting, standing, and walking. Language begins with movement, gurgling, and cooing and progresses to single words and two-word phrases.[19] The mark of this particular turning point in a child's development is the acquisition of one particular simple word and its meaning—"No!"

Ages 2–6: The Child Who Stands beside Jesus

The child who can say, "No!" and mean it has begun to develop a sense of self as being autonomous from objects and other persons. Parenting of children at this stage of development is a process of letting go in a very real sense. Parents let the child go as he or she attempts to stand and move, yet they are there to pick the child up if he or she falls. Adults in the child's environment have to balance nurturing the child's autonomy by creating space for making mistakes and learning with stepping in to assist when the child is frustrated by the inability to perform a desired task. Perhaps caregivers need to follow Jesus' example of placing the child *alongside* him by staying within children's reach and allowing them to guide adult intervention.

In addition to autonomy, early childhood sees the advent of symbolic language. The child who has developed object constancy no longer needs to have the object or person present, but can call it by name. The child uses language to make sense out of the amazing array of things in the physical environment. When a new object, person, or animal enters his or her space the young child will try to make sense of it from within previously acquired categories and notions. Piaget called this attempt at categorization "assimilation." When a child cannot fit an existing object or person into the existing categories, a process called "accommodation" takes place in which the child adapts internal structures to accommodate the new object or person. The following account illustrates the processes of assimilation and accommodation in preschoolers.

> I often use rhythm instruments when teaching music with preschoolers. We begin our explorations by sitting in a circle and placing the instruments in the center one by one as they are named. I start with

a small array of instruments, most of which would be found in any preschool setting—things like maracas, tambourines, drums, and rhythm sticks. As we continue our journey into music education, I gradually add less familiar instruments to the center of the circle. We then begin looking for the commonalities between the instruments by considering questions such as: From what material is the unfamiliar instrument made? How is it played? What other instruments are played in the same way? In this way the unfamiliar instrument is assimilated into existing categories of what it means to play a musical instrument.

Occasionally I will add an instrument that does not fit into existing categories, such as a blue accordion-pleated plastic tube that is larger at one end. Without identifying this instrument I let the children try to figure out how it is played. Most will try to blow it because it resembles a wind instrument in some ways, but blowing produces no noise. Someone usually figures out that you can twirl it around and around to produce a sound. This is a new way of playing an instrument that must be accommodated by creating a new category for twirled instruments.

Not only are children aged two to six attuned to the world they can see in their environments, they are also creating worlds in their imaginations that only they can see. I recently had a conversation with a four-year-old before a trip to the zoo, in which he told me that the animal he most wanted to see was a porcupine. Intrigued that a four-year-old would even be aware of such an uncommon animal, I asked him if he had ever seen a porcupine. In reply, he launched into a lengthy, detailed story about an encounter with a porcupine in which he was stuck by the quills. He also informed me that if he sat in a certain tree and some special liquid potion was poured into his right ear, he could become a porcupine. Had the child ever seen a porcupine? Not according to his parents, who were puzzled and amused by the conversation. Perhaps he had heard a story in which a porcupine was the dominant character. This incident highlights the powerful images that are created within preschool children's minds and the range of emotions that are exhibited through their narratives. James Fowler points out the power of narratives to spark preschool children's imaginations and to allow them to process fears and anxieties.[20] Fowler suggests that biblical narratives are particularly suited for this purpose—hence the perennial popularity of stories like Daniel in the lion's den and the overseeing of the baby Moses by his sister, Miriam.

By telling stories of our faith to young children, we provide narratives with great power to transform fear to hope. Storytelling also provides the language of faith—familiar characters and religious vocabulary—that will serve them through adulthood. Some people advise against telling Bible stories before children have the capacity to plumb the depths of their meaning, but studying the stories later in life would be like learning a second language rather than drawing on images and faith material that were appropriate early in childhood. As children grow and hear the stories again and again, they can add the layers of complexity of meaning in concert with developing capacities and cognitive abilities.

By placing themselves in stories, children between the ages of two and six see the world of their imaginations through their own egocentric perspective. This type of imaginative play also allows children to explore the concepts of life and death and the rituals that surround them. Much of my own work centers around talking to children about death and watching their play of death. Many preschoolers will develop games in which one child dies and the others hold a funeral. Some children will pretend to be mummies and come back from the dead. After September 11, 2001, many children began building towers and knocking them down. In cases of actual loss, many children will believe that they hold the power life and death and that if they were able to change their own actions or perform new ones, they would be able to bring the person who has died back to life.[21]

Jerome Berryman, an Episcopal priest and Christian educator, taps into this world of imaginative and ritualistic play in his work in *Godly Play: An Imaginative Approach to Religious Education* (Minneapolis: Augsburg, 1991). In Berryman's approach, the classroom is transformed into a liturgical play space where children are invited to enter the world of a parable or other biblical text and respond to that encounter through art, storytelling, or exploration. The adventure ends with a ritualistic feast akin to communion. Berryman's method responds to a child's natural sense of wonder, exploration, and ritual and provides an avenue for religious conversations between preschoolers and caregivers. Berryman draws heavily on the work of Howard Gardner and Maria Montessori, two cultural developmentalists.

Just as Piaget and Freud were foundational to classic developmental theories, Maria Montessori and Lev Vygotsky serve as foundations for cultural theories of preschool development. Even though a few cultural theories begin with the child under the age of two, (notably that of Montessori), the primary emphasis is about age two when language emerges and cultural differences become more pronounced. Emphasis on the role of the child's environment in development sets these theories apart from those of classic developmentalists.

Maria Montessori, an Italian physician and educational philosopher, is often viewed as an educator but is seldom given credit for her developmental theory. Montessori's work serves as a bridge between classic and cultural developmentalists. With the classic developmentalists, she believes that there is genetic material within children that determines universal aspects of development. In Montessori's understanding, all children go through a progression of sensitive periods, "genetically programmed blocks of time during which the child is especially eager and able to master certain tasks."[22] Sensitive periods begin in infancy and relate to the need for order, a sensitivity to detail, the use of hands and feet, and the acquisition of language. For Montessori, language acquisition is almost an imprinting or absorption of sounds and vocabulary from the environment before the child actually uses the language. The language acquisition mechanism, which people lose as they age, allows children to acquire language and underlying grammatical structures unconsciously and at a much more rapid rate than adults. This unconscious language acquisition ends at about age three, but children remain in a language-sensitive period until age six. This description of language acquisition supports the need for early exposure to religious language and imagery.

Montessori regarded the role of parents as one of walking alongside the child as his or her first educators, allowing the expression of personal interests and providing the opportunity to explore them. For instance, as a child learns to walk and wants to explore, parents walk at the child's pace, stop when the child stops, and explore what the child is interested in. Montessori faulted parents for thinking like adults when approaching children. For example, during the sensitive period of walking, many parents will assume that children walk to get someplace, as adults do, so to serve that end they will pick the child up or transport the child in a stroller. Yet, for children in this sensitive period, walking is a way of testing the power of their legs and muscles, so they walk simply to practice walking. Parents may fear that their children will wander too far or get into harm's way, so they use playpens and gates for protection, although these things hinder children's ability to explore their new abilities and their independence.

Montessori believed in creating safe learning environments that allow autonomy and freedom of choice while providing rich activities that engage the mind of the child. Her most extensive work was done with children ages two to six. Montessori and others like Sofia Cavaletti who have applied her educational methods were Roman Catholic and believed that religious symbols and language should be included in the child's learning environment. This may be why many churches house Montessori schools. Children in Montessori schools are encouraged to independently master the skills for which they are sensitively attuned by their development. Children choose activities and often work on them with extreme concentration. These tasks represent small steps on the way to fine motor and discrimination skills that will serve them in complex tasks such as reading and writing and in tasks of independence such as tying shoes and buttoning sweaters. By being provided an environment that has been organized with rich and varied activities, the preschool child is encouraged to find his or her own rewards in accomplishing a selected task. In Montessori's approach, the educator, plays the role of guide and observer, responding to the child's sense of discovery and encouraging each attempt at a new task.

What insight does Montessori offer for the development of faith? A definition of faith as active practicing seems to be at play in Montessori's approach. In recent years, a number of theological educators have been exploring the nature of faith practices and their implications for Christian education.[23] These practices include hospitality, saying yes and saying no, keeping Sabbath, testimony, shaping communities, forgiveness, healing, singing,[24] and honoring the body, all of which are accessible to young children. Montessori's developmental theory and educational philosophy offer support for a faith-practicing approach with preschoolers.

Below are example of activities that provide developmentally appropriate opportunities for two- to six-year-olds to engage in the faith practice of honoring the body.

- Preschoolers are fascinated by their own bodies and those of their peers. Tasks of discrimination and valuing will help children celebrate and appreciate differences in height, weight, hair, skin and eye color, and clothing styles. Creating an environment where children celebrate cultural and physical differences will allow for the faith practices of hospitality and shaping communities to be more successful.

- Another component of the faith practice of honoring the body is using the body to worship God. This component can be broken down into small increments with preschoolers practicing different stances of worship and prayer, such as sitting, standing, kneeling, and lying down. Through song, children can explore quiet and noisy ways of using their mouths and voices to worship God.
- Children can also learn how to pass the peace as a way of understanding appropriate touch between persons.
- Preschoolers can use touch to become familiar with objects of worship such as the cross, cup and plate, stoles and robes, hymnbooks and Bibles, and the baptismal font and water.
- The Bible is full of passages that lift up the body: in the creation story, where God's breath creates the world; in the New Testament accounts of Jesus' birth and death, and in the resurrection appearances, where Jesus asks the disciples to touch the wounds in his hands and side. Teachers can help preschoolers relate to this bodily sense of woundedness and healing touch by reminding them of when their parents feel their foreheads to check for fever or kiss their "boo-boos" when they are hurt.

As can be seen from the examples for honoring the body, the faith practices have rich potential for early childhood education. Montessori's method of structuring the environment with small tasks that lead to maturity in various skills offers insight for introducing faith practices.

Another theory intended as a bridge between cultural developmental and classical developmental theories is that of Russian psychologist, Lev Semenovich Vygotsky. A contemporary of Piaget, Vygotsky was well-acquainted with the classic theories of the time, but until the breakup of the Soviet Union in the late twentieth-century, much of his work remained unknown in the West. Vygotsky's basic premise was that certain aspects of development, like the object separation, are universal, but as a child matures, cultural factors are developed—such as language, numbering systems, and abstract thinking—that vary according to the cultural technology of a given people. Just as different physical tools become dominant in various groups, Vygotsky believed that different psychological tools also dominate a given culture. For instance, different cultures develop different cues to aid the memory. Remembering the faith may involve setting up stones as in ancient Hebrew culture or reciting answers to catechisms as in historical and contemporary Christian cultures.

Vygotsky believed that the preschool years in particular were critical for developing psychological tools, especially the tool of speech. He was expressly interested in speech as a cultural sign that aided individuals in reflecting on personal actions.[25] Vygotsky saw the development of "internal dialogue" as a threefold process where the child first begins speaking about absent objects with the prompting of others. To illustrate, a mother asks her daughter to get her offering money and Bible for church. The child responds by retrieving the objects not in view. Next, the child begins speaking the words out loud to herself—a stage of the process that begins at about age three—"We are going to church. I need my Bible and offering money." By the age of eight this "internal dialogue," as Vygotsky terms it, or "egocentric speech" to use Piaget's terminology, becomes internalized to the point that it is now inner speech, heard only by the child. When it is time for church, the child will internally prompt herself to retrieve the necessary tools for this cultural context.

Vygotsky and later researchers also looked at internal dialogue as something that is related to the moral behavior of children. Willpower is thought to begin with promptings from others in the child's environment, then to be vocalized during the preschool years, and, finally, internalized. Adults often find themselves in situations in which they struggle. These situations call for internal verbalizations, which help adults take desired actions. For instance, many people find it difficult to maintain a time for spiritual devotion in the midst of life's competing demands. Vygotsky would suggest that those people who could internally vocalize limits to their behavior, such as, "I am going to get up at 6:00 AM instead of 6:30 AM in order to have time to devote to Bible study and prayer each morning," would be more successful directing their willpower to the desired goal. According to Vygotsky, the critical period of ages two to six is when children learn to regulate behavior through these verbal, cultural cues.

Vygotsky was also one of the first developmentalists to link theory to schooling. Vygotsky saw a much more active role for the teacher than did Montessori. He believed that there are skills that children acquire naturally, but he also believed that simply creating the learning environment is not enough. In Vygotsky's view, certain skills, including abstract thinking, are acquired only in a school setting that emphasizes training in symbolic disciplines such as writing and number systems. He calls the zone between what a child naturally learns and what a child is able to accomplish with the aid of a gifted teacher the "zone of proximal development."[26] This zone varies between individuals in a given culture and may aid teachers in assessing the potential learning of each child.

In recent years, many educators/developmentalists have applied Vygotsky's theories in various ways.[27] One of the most comprehensive applications of Vygotsky's work by an American has been the work of David Henry Feldman of Tufts University. In his book *Beyond Cognitive Universals* (Norwood, NJ: Ablex Publishing, 1980), Feldman divides the different abilities that individuals acquire into different levels of development. These abilities range from those skills that are universal—crossing all cultural boundaries—to abilities that are unique within individuals who are deemed geniuses in a given domain within a particular culture. For example, within the Western cultural heritage, Einstein in science, Picasso in art, Mozart in music, and Martin Luther King, and Mother Teresa in spirituality/interpersonal skills might be considered geniuses in the domains they represent. In between these two extremes of universal development of all and unique development of a limited few lie skills that are developed because a culture values them (such as, cooking or navigation), or more abstract skills that would be taught directly in schools (such as, the academic disciplines). What Feldman's system points out is that a child does not develop entirely in isolation but is dependent on the surrounding culture to identify valued skills and provide training in an apprentice fashion or through formal schooling.

To illustrate: Tying shoes is a skill that is valued in American culture. How do children learn to tie shoes? Shoe tying is not something children naturally acquire in isolation. Without observing others, it would be difficult to know the purpose of the shoelace or that the desired outcome is a correctly tied bow. Most preschoolers first observe others tying shoes, then come to a point when they desire to learn the skill. A master shoe tier will then provide step-by-step instruction, followed by the child apprentice attempting the tying process with the guidance of the master tier. Eventually the child will learn to tie shoes and then can be a master for other apprentices.

What does this have to do with faith? The similarity can be illustrated by considering one of the cultural skills that Christians expect children to acquire in order to become mature in the faith, namely prayer. Even the youngest child learns quickly that for most people, praying means that the head is bowed, the eyes are closed, and the hands are folded. It is easy for children to copy the physical postures that they see in their faith culture, but is this what praying is about? It is only through the guidance of someone with a mature faith (a master prayer, as it were) that the child can learn what it means to carry on a dialogue with God. As an apprentice, the child first says prayers aloud at mealtimes, before bed, and in various settings at church. After awhile the apprentice prayer can be encouraged to say prayers internally and to experiment with other prayer postures, so that as in the words of the apostle Paul, the child can pray in all circumstances without ceasing (1 Thess. 5:16–18).

Building on the work of Vygotsky and Feldman, Howard Gardner has combined this view of development with neurological and cultural research to develop his theory of multiple intelligences. This theory has become very popular within educational circles.[28] For purposes of this discussion, only two aspects of Gardner's theory will be highlighted: Gardner and his associates' research in the area of preschool education and Gardner's musings on a definition of "spiritual intelligence."

In Project Zero, a grant-funded educational research project affiliated with Harvard's Graduate School of Education, research that focused on preschool education that truly addresses individual difference was begun in the early 1990s. Just as fingerprints differ, so do persons' intelligence profiles. Grounded in multiple intelligences theory, Project Spectrum, one of the projects conducted by Project Zero researchers, was born to design intelligence-fair assessments for the purpose of determining the strengths and weaknesses of a given child's intelligence profile. For instance, one child might show evidence of strong potentials in the areas of musical, linguistic, and interpersonal intelligences, while another child might show signs of strength in logical-mathematical, spatial, and bodily-kinesthetic intelligences. The researchers wanted to be able to structure tasks that would fairly assess each of the intelligences.[29]

One observation from Project Spectrum is that children gravitate to particular activities in their strong domains and, when faced with a task or assessment in a weaker domain, often bring to bear their strengths, as the following examples illustrate.

- Seth, who enjoyed storytelling, transformed the sink and float activity into a story about the "great and famous sponge man."

• Sarah transported her language skills to the art table by making decorative drawings for the stories she invented.[30]

This reveals the importance of training teachers in Christian education programs to be observers of children's potential intelligence profiles. Many Christian educational events offer preschoolers a time when they can choose from a selection of activities. By noting what preferences children show during these times, teachers can select educational tools that use children's strengths to guide them into a deeper understanding of a biblical story or theological concept.

Gardner sees this type of education as a bridge between models in which the curriculum is based mainly on the child's interest and models in which the process is highly directed by an adult. Like Montessori's method, Gardner's Spectrum model is based on active involvement, individualized education, and a "prepared" environment, but Gardner suggests that this model offers more room for creativity in the use of materials. This is similar to project-based models based on the work of Piaget and Dewey in which small groups of preschool children work intensively on a particular project that involves knowledge, skills, working styles, and feelings.

One other component of the Project Spectrum methodology that is worth consideration by Christian educators of preschoolers is the partnership that the various children's centers developed with the Boston Children's Museum.[31] Gardner had already identified children's museums as models of education that excite children to explore and be creative.[32] The partnership with the museum consisted of regularly scheduled field trips to the museum and coordination of fundamental concepts and themes in the preschool and museum curricula. The museum provided follow-up packets so that the children could continue the exploration in their home environments.

A recent visit to the Jewish Museum in New York City convinced me that exciting experiences at museums can be created for children within a given religious tradition.[33] Organized around four recurring themes of Judaism—covenant, land, law, and exodus—the museum offers visitors a journey through exhibits of historical artifacts, auditory and visual experiences of ritual practices, interactive assessment of knowledge, and viewpoints of issues concerning Jews. The reader is invited to spend some time thinking about what a Christian children's museum might look like. What major themes of the faith would be highlighted? What historical artifacts would tell the story of

Christianity through the ages? What rituals would children need to experience? What perplexing issues would be addressed, and what sources for decision making would be recommended? What are the practical issues involved in housing such an institution? Would it be possible to devote church space for such a project, or would a regional governing body be able to house such a center in partnership with local churches? Are theological institutions the place for an experimental museum where research on children's faith explorations could be carried out in partnership with local educators? The potential for faith development in a museum of Christianity is considerable for those willing to explore the possibilities.

Children aged two to six are excited about learning. This is an important period in children's development in general and faith development in particular. Developmental theories offer rich insights for nurturing faith development. Faith can be said to develop in infancy as trust in something beyond one's self or a sense of transcendence.[34] Young children's first images of God may be a combination of the images they have of their caretakers and influences with which they have come into contact during infancy. Symbolic language, the play of ritual, and the culture of the church community all affect a child's growing faith. Yet, the outstanding question remains: "What exactly is faith?"

Receiving the Kingdom of God

> People were bringing even infants to him that he might touch them; and when the disciples saw it, they sternly ordered them not to do it. But Jesus called for them and said, "Let the little children come to me, and do not stop them; for it is to such as these that the kingdom of God belongs. Truly I tell you, whoever does not receive the kingdom of God as a little child will never enter it" (Luke 18:15–17).

Two developmentalists who have taken on the definition of faith are James Fowler, who represents the classic developmental school, and Howard Gardner, a cultural developmentalist.

When James Fowler's *Stages of Faith* reached religious communities back in 1981, educators were the first to accept this radical way of viewing the faith process. After all, for years Christian educators had appropriated the work of Jean Piaget, Lawrence Kohlberg, Erik Erikson, and others for writing curriculum resources and designing educational experiences. The territory covered in Fowler's work, which drew on recognized theories and was based on extensive faith interviews with persons of a variety of ages, was familiar to Christian educators.

For Fowler, faith is a response, an action rather than a set of doctrines to be learned.[35] Faith is relational in a triadic way among God, the self, and others. Faith is imaginative, forcing persons to create images of relations beyond the usual human kind. Faith also forms identity. As people develop in relationship beyond themselves, they know more clearly who they are. Faith development, then, becomes a series of stages that moves persons further into mature relationship and into faith identity. These stages correspond to many of the stage divisions of the classical theories. As with classical theories, Fowler's stages are thought to be sequential and consistent for all peoples and religions. There are characteristics and transitional signs that signal a move from one stage to the next. Fowler sees ages three to seven, at which stage children experience what he refers to as Intuitive-Projective faith, as a time of perception and imagination when faith constructions and images are not constrained by logical thought.[36] Fowler cautions that faith images and feelings formed during this time have long-lasting impacts on a child, youth, or adult's maturing faith.

Howard Gardner wrestles with the concept of a broad definition of faith under the banner of a possible "spiritual intelligence."[37] Keeping with his theory of multiple intelligences, Gardner attempts to define a spiritual intelligence that can be subject to neurological and psychological testing. He also looks for people who would be considered prodigies (maturing more rapidly than expected in spiritual matters), or savants (those who are exceptional in spiritual matters but are weak in most of the other intelligences). For Gardner, an intelligence must have a core set of defined operations that a person can perform. There must be an identifiable end state, and the intelligence must have a symbol system distinct from other intelligences. Can spirituality fit all these criteria?

Gardner's biggest problem came in trying to determine exactly what it means to be spiritual. He explored three different possibilities that cross religious boundaries:

1. Spiritual as concern with cosmic or existential issues, which concerns individuals who spend considerable time pondering life's mysteries and big questions, such as "Who are we?" "Why do we exist?" "What is the meaning of life and death?" (It is difficult to imagine a preschool prodigy who would spend much time in this way, but it is possible.)

2. Spiritual as achievement of a state of being, which involves two kinds of knowing—*knowing how* and *knowing that*.[38] *Knowing how* might be defined as a set of behaviors used to reach an altered consciousness that involves some type of transcendence. *Knowing that* might consist of mastering the content of a given faith. Gardner rejects this definition of faith because it is too value laden and culturally specific to be studied scientifically in an interfaith fashion.

3. Spiritual as effect on others, which consists of singling out some of the acknowledged geniuses from different faith traditions and looking for commonalities in the ways they have influenced others. "Geniuses" include Mother Teresa, Martin Luther King, Jr., and Mahatma Gandhi. Gardner even suggests, but ultimately rejects, looking at commonalities in how historical religious leaders such as Buddha, Christ, Mohammed, and Confucius approached faith and influenced disciples. Gardner's rejection came because this proposal does not fit his definition of intelligence as "problem solving" or "product making."

So it would seem that the first definition of spirituality as existentiality is the only one that will fit within Gardner's theory. Gardner himself, although declining any personal involvement in spiritual issues, is not willing to reduce spirituality to pondering life's mysteries, so at most he is willing to acknowledge existentiality as possibly a half of an intelligence.[39] Scientific evidence is sparse if at all extant in this area. This leaves open the question of ways of knowing that go beyond the observable and measurable world of cognitive psychology.

Discussion of attempts by developmentalists to define faith points out the limits of a developmental perspective for looking at issues of faith and necessarily leads to the question of whether or not it is appropriate to propose developmental definitions. Craig Dykstra, former professor at Princeton Theological Seminary and current Vice-President of Religion at the Lilly Foundation, points to several aspects of the developmental perspective that run counter to traditions within Christianity and therefore preclude defining faith in developmental terms.[40]

• First, theories of human development presuppose human initiative as the impetus to growth and change. This doesn't leave much room for God's initiative, which is part of the Reformed theological heritage. How do we reconcile definitions of faith that have their basis in human action with the grace of God that is proclaimed in Scripture? "For by grace you have been saved through faith, and this is not your own doing; it is the gift of God" (Eph. 2:8).

- Second, theories of human development do not take seriously the power of sin and evil to derail "normal" human progress through the developmental stages. What impact do tragic life events have on a child's faith? How would the death of parents or other family members affect images of God that are being formed at an early age? What do poverty, racism, and other social evils do to a child's growing faith and trust?

- Third, theories of human development do not address the impact of individual differences, such as learning styles and disabilities, on universal faith development stages? Even without tragedy, life experience and God's unique relationship with each person suggest faith growth that differs with each person. Just as siblings within a family have differing relationships with their parents, so do Christians experience the ongoing presence and guidance of Christ in different ways. There are many other questions to be asked about the particularity of developmental theories and defining faith development, which point to a complex picture of faith.

- Finally, the particularity of the new life in Christ makes universalizing theories alien and restrictive to the actual discipleship experience. Both the classic and cultural views of development paint the picture of faith in broad strokes designed to be inclusive of a variety of religious belief. What difference does the Christian experience make in defining the faith of young children? Does the fact that Jesus welcomed rather than excluded children mean that infants, toddlers, and preschoolers also experience Christian discipleship?

There are aspects of Christianity, then, that necessitate taking a critical look at development theory as a basis for defining faith. Dykstra defines the problem in this way:

> The issue is not how much or how fast we grow but in what context. . . . Coming to faith means coming to recognize that the context of all our growing and living is the world in which, over which, and through which the Spirit of God known in Jesus Christ reigns.[41]

Does the act of faith then negate human development? James Loder, former Mary D. Wynott Chair of Philosophy of Christian

Education at Princeton Theological Seminary, had given this idea considerable thought. Loder saw human development psychologies and the theological understanding of the Holy Spirit as working together much as the divine and human natures of Christ relate to each other.[42] In our traditional understanding, Christ was fully human and fully divine at the same time. So we as humans are fully human and in relationship with a fully divine, triune God. This "relational unity" is the interaction of the Holy Spirit with our human spirits. In the midst of this relationship are moments of transformation when humans are conformed more fully with Christ.[43] Transformation can happen at any age. As indicated earlier in this chapter, the first experience with the transcendent may be the realization that the mother (or other caregiver who is primarily responsible for feeding the infant) is separate from the self. Looking at the face of the mother who gives all good gifts to the child may be like looking at the face of God, the Giver of all good gifts. As the child develops autonomy of ego and learns the word "No!" his or her human spirit becomes separate from the "yes" of the mother's face. It is the Holy Spirit working through this image of the divine face that, according to Loder, will bring about transformation within the infant by negating the child's "No" with the divine "Yes," which releases young children to soar above the limits of a developmental perspective.[44] So from this perspective, human development and faith can work together in the child's life, with the working of the Holy Spirit, allowing faith to override the constraints of what it means to be human.

Welcoming the Child

When does faith begin? Theological and developmental perspectives both suggest that faith begins when life begins. The remaining question, then, is: *What does a reading of human development from a faith perspective mean for the church in its ministry with young children?*

Some of the practical applications of the various theories have been noted throughout this chapter and bear revisiting. For children under the age of two, the need for consistent caregivers who provide the necessities, yet allow enough space for the child to exert growing independence, are essential. There are implications, then, for staffing a church nursery, such as, will there be paid workers or rotating volunteers? There are also implications for training people who desire to work with our youngest believers.[45] The writings of Jerome Berryman, Maria Montessori, and Howard Gardner all suggest structuring educational programs for children ages two to six that reflect the current emphasis on faith practices. Developmental theories also have specific implications for ministry with children in worship, preschool programs, and the home.

Each congregation will need to address the following questions at some point:[46]

- Are children welcomed and encouraged to participate in worship?
- What preparation for the worship experience is offered to parents and children?
- What tools does your church make available on Sunday morning to help the children understand and participate in worship?
- How do children participate in the service? Do they stay through the whole worship service? If not, what type of faith formation is going on when they are absent from worship?

Developmental theories can be used as support for allowing children in worship to overhear and observe the faith, to develop faith practices, to cultivate rich images of God, and to experience the transcendence of the collective body worshiping something beyond itself. Developmental theories can also guide the creation of a separate time of faith formation in which a child could use active learning to engage the objects and rituals of faith. It will take God's gift of discernment for congregations to determine where the Holy Spirit can best work with young children in their context.

Infants and toddlers may spend the worship time in the church nursery. Note has been made of the important role of trained caregivers in forming first images of transcendence and trust. Attention also has been drawn to the work of Karen Marie Yust as it relates to "overhearing" and "overseeing" the faith.[45] There are implications here for having audio or video access to the worship service in the church nursery.[47] Again, it is important to remember that children up through age two acquire language through movement and internalization before it is expressed.

The impact of visual images as well as auditory stimuli is an important consideration for the nursery environment. Are there colorful pictures of people engaged in various faith practices hung at the child's eye level in the nursery? Are there simple picture books with biblical characters and faith symbols? Do any of the toys or objects in the nursery have faith meanings? It is critical to provide intentional exposure to the faith culture of the community in the space where infants and toddlers spend most of their time.

Churches that have preschools also need to ask questions such as: What is the relationship of the school to the church's ministry? Is spiritual and faith development evident in the curriculum along with cognitive, social, language, and emotional development? Is the church willing to look on the children in the preschool as members of the faith community in the same way as those who participate in Sunday events?

The church also has a responsibility to minister to the home life of young children. Parent education and encouragement of family devotional time can be part of the church's educational program. The faith practices may be helpful in this context as well. A unit on the faith practice of household economics, for instance, may allow families to plan for a simpler lifestyle that includes time to gather together in a family worship time. A good resource for families in the PC(USA) is the catechetical resource titled *We Are the Family of God* (Sally Johnson and Ann Reed Held, Presbyterian Publishing Corporation, 1998), which allows families to work through the *Belonging to God* catechism in a devotional way. This material also allows the family to plan action as faith response. As suggested by the cultural school of developmental theory, children are not driven entirely by innate universal development. The culture surrounding children shapes their faith practices and beliefs. It is not enough to teach children in age-specific Sunday school classrooms; parents need the church to work in partnership with them in educating their children in the faith.

When does faith begin? Within Christianity and in the Reformed tradition in particular, we would say that faith begins when God initiates a relationship with the individual believer. It is evident from developmental theories that this relationship can begin very early in life. With a trustworthy environment, caring models of faithful believers, intentional nurture of faith practices, and sensitivity to the uniqueness of individual capabilities, the relationship between Christ and the young child can grow and flourish. The child in Scripture stands beside Jesus, just as the collective body of children today stand by the church. The church has the opportunity to invite children to become full members of the body of Christ and to delight in their enlivening presence.

NOTES

1. Gerhard Kittell and Gerhard Friedrich, eds., *Theological Dictionary of the New Testament,* trans. Geoffrey W. Bromiley, vol. V, s.v. (Grand Rapids: Eerdmans, 1976), 637–638.

2. Feldman, David Henry, *Beyond Universals in Cognitive Development,* 2nd ed. (Norwood, NJ: Ablex Publishing, 1994), 20–21.

3. Recent advances in brain research confirm the importance of the first year, months, and even weeks of life. The videotape *I Am Your Child: The First Years Last Forever* provides a good introduction to the topic. It is available from the I Am Your Child Foundation c/o TASCO, Inc., 9 Jay Gould Court, Waldorf, MA 20602, phone (310) 285–2385.

4. Jean Piaget and Bärbel Inhelder, *The Psychology of the Child.* trans. Helen Weaver (New York: Basic Books, 1969), 7.

5. Robert Kegan, *The Evolving Self: Problem and Process in Human Development* (Cambridge, MA: Harvard University Press, 1982), 30.

6. Ibid., 31.

7. "Object Relations Theory" in *Dictionary of Pastoral Care and Counseling,* Rodney J. Hunter, ed. (Nashville: Abingdon Press, 1990), 796.

8. D. W. Winnicott, *Playing and Reality.* (London: Routledge, 1996), 3.

9. The "good-enough mother" is a term developed by D. W. Winnicott, by which he meant an ordinary woman whose maternal instincts are not deflected by her own disabilities or by so-called expert advice and who protects her infant from the primitive anxieties.

10. James W. Jones, "Playing and Believing: The Uses of D. W. Winnicott in the Psychology of Religion," in *Religion, Society, and Psychoanalysis: Readings in Contemporary Theory*, ed. Janet Liebman Jacobs and Donald Capps (Boulder, CO: Westview, 1997), 113.

11. Ibid., 112.

12. Ana-Maria Rizzuto, *The Birth of the Living God: A Psychoanalytic Study* (Chicago: University of Chicago Press, 1979), 206.

13. Erik H. Erikson, *Childhood and Society* (New York: W. W. Norton, [1950] 1993), 247.

14. Ibid., 248.

15. Ibid., 250–251.

16. James W. Fowler proposes a primal faith that precedes his stage theory, and addresses this affect in *Stages of Faith: The Psychology of Human Development and the Quest for Meaning* (San Francisco: Harper, 1981), 119–121.

17. Many researchers agree that separation anxiety from the primary caregiver begins at around ten months, peaks at twelve months, and ceases at about twenty-one months. Kegan, *The Evolving Self,* 81.

18. Even though object constancy develops at an early age, even as adults we often fear separation from our Provider. This is evident in the psalms of lament, in Job, and in other places that express the fear of God's absence.

19. The work of Noam Chomsky is especially helpful for understanding this innate sequence of language development. A good synopsis of his work, including a discussion of his concept of an underlying "universal grammar" that is broad enough to encompass cultural linguistic difference, can be found in William Crain, *Theories of Development: Concepts and Applications*, 3rd ed. (Englewood Cliffs, NJ: Prentice Hall, 1992), 299–316.

20. Fowler, *Stages of Faith*, 130.

21. Gerri L. Sweder, "Talking to Children about the Terminal Illness of a Loved One," in *Bereaved Children and Teens: A Support Guide for Parents and Professionals*, ed. Earl A. Grollman (Boston: Beacon Press, 1995), 49. See also Ponette, videocassette with subtitles, 92 min., Les Films Alain Sarde/Rhone-Alpes Cinema, France, 1996.

22. Crain, *Theories of Development*, 59.

23. See in particular Dorothy C. Bass, ed., *Practicing Our Faith: A Way of Life for a Searching People* (San Francisco: Jossey-Bass Publishers, 1997) and Craig Dykstra, *Growing in the Life of Faith: Education and Christian Practices* (Louisville: Geneva Press, 1999). Also Dorothy C. Bass and Don Richter, *Way to Live: Christian Practices for Teens* (Nashville: Upper Room Books, 2002). See web site: www.practicingyourfaith.com for further information.

24. Chapter titles found in Dorothy C. Bass, ed., *Practicing Our Faith: A Way of Life for a Searching People* (San Francisco: Jossey-Bass Publishers, 1997)

25. Crain, *Theories of Development*, 201–210.

26. Ibid., 214.

27. Harry Daniels, ed., *Charting the Agenda: Educational Activity after Vygotsky* (London: Routledge, 1994); Michael Cole and James V. Wertsch, *Contemporary Implications of Vygotsky and Luria* (Worcester, MA: Clark University Press, 1996).

28. Those not familiar with the basic premises of the theory may want to skim Chapter three of this resource before continuing through the next few paragraphs.

29. Many testing measures that purport to test individual intelligences rely heavily on reading and writing to demonstrate competence in other areas, so in actuality it is the child's linguistic abilities that are being tested rather than the content of the desired discipline.

30. Jie-Qi Chen, Mara Krechevsky and Julie Viens, *Building on Children's Strengths: The Experience of Project Spectrum* (New York: Teachers College Press, 1998), 28.

31. Ibid., 73–84.

32. Howard Gardner, *The Unschooled Mind* (New York: Basic Books, 1991), 13, 202.

33. Jewish Museum, 1109 Fifth Avenue, New York, NY 10128. Phone: (212) 423-3200; Web site: www.jewishmuseum.org.

34. One resource on faith as transcendence in young children is Barbara Kimes Myers and William R. Myers, *Engaging in Transcendence: The Church's Ministry and Covenant with Young Children* (Cleveland: Pilgrim Press, 1992).

35. Fowler, *Stages of Faith,* 33.

36. Ibid., 133.

37. Howard Gardner, "Are There Additional Intelligences?" in *Intelligence Reframed: Multiple Intelligences for the 21st Century* (New York: Basic Books, 1999), 47–66.

38. Ibid., 55.

39. Ibid., 64.

40. Dykstra, *Growing in the Life of Faith*, 37.

41. Ibid.

42. Loder identifies this relationship as the Chalcedonian formula, going back to the early church council that made a determination of the ortho-dox understanding of Jesus' full humanity and full divinity. James Loder, *The Logic of the Spirit: Human Development in Theological Perspective* (San Francisco: Jossey-Bass, 1998), 37.

43. Ibid., 41.

44. Ibid., 110.

45. Even before language is expressed, infants are beginning to form images of God, to learn to trust those around them, and to absorb the cul-ture of the church that surrounds them. Karen Marie Yust, assistant profes-sor of Christian Education at Christian Theological Seminary in Indianapolis, Indiana, refers to this phenomenon in infants and toddlers as "overhearing" or "overseeing" the faith. Dr. Yust currently heads research called the Faith Formation in Children's Ministries Project, which contacts churches that are doing significant work in children's ministry throughout the country in hopes of identifying best practices for ministry with children. For more information on the project, see Karen Marie Yust's faculty page on the Web at www.cts.edu.

46. There are many resources to aid churches in thinking through the place of children in worship, including Herbert Anderson and Susan B. W. Johnson, *Regarding Children: A New Respect for Childhood and Families* (Louisville: Westminster/John Knox, 1994); Sara Covin Juengst, *Sharing Faith with Children: Rethinking the Children's Sermon* (Louisville: Westminster/John Knox, 1994); Jean Floyd Love et al., *Get Ready, Get Set, Worship!: A Resource for Including Children in Worship* (Louisville: Geneva Press, 1998); and Elizabeth Caldwell, *Come Unto Me: Rethinking the Sacraments for Children* (Cleveland: United Church Press, 1996).

47. This was an example used by Karen Marie Yust when explaining her concepts to a group of childhood educators and researchers at the Association for Professors and Researchers in Religious Education confer-ence in Atlanta, November 2000.

DEVELOPMENTAL BIBLIOGRAPHY (SELECTED)

Bass, Dorothy C., ed., *Practicing Our Faith: A Way of Life for a Searching People*. San Francisco: Jossey-Bass Publishers, 1997.

Crain, William. *Theories of Development: Concepts and Applications*. Third Edition. Englewood Cliffs, NJ: Prentice Hall, 1992.

Dykstra, Craig. *Growing in the Life of Faith: Education and Christian Practices*. Louisville, KY: Geneva Press, 1999.

Erikson, Erik H. *Childhood and Society*. New York: W. W. Norton [1950], 1993.

Feldman, David Henry. *Beyond Universals in Cognitive Development*, 2nd ed. Norwood, NJ: Ablex Publishing, 1994.

Fowler, James W. *Stages of Faith: The Psychology of Human Development and the Quest for Meaning*. San Francisco: Harper, 1981.

Gardner, Howard. *The Quest for Mind: Piaget, Levi-Strauss and the Structuralist Movement*. New York: Vintage Books, 1972.

————. *The Unschooled Mind: How Children Think and How Schools Should Teach*. New York: Basic Books, 1991.

————. *Intelligence Reframed: Multiple Intelligences for the 21st Century*. New York: Basic Books, 1999.

Kegan, Robert. *The Evolving Self: Problem and Process in Human Development*. Cambridge, MA: Harvard University Press, 1982.

Loder, James E. *The Logic of the Spirit: Human Development in Theological Perspective*. San Francisco: Jossey-Bass, 1998.

Piaget, Jean and Bärbel Inhelder. *The Psychology of the Child*, Translated by Helen Weaver. New York: Basic Books, 1969.

Rizzuto, Ana-Maria. *The Birth of the Living God: A Psychoanalytic Study*. Chicago: University of Chicago Press, 1979.

CHAPTER THREE

Multiple Intelligences Theory and Ministry with Children

Joyce MacKichan Walker and
Carol A. Wehrheim

Multiple Intelligences Theory: What It Is

Being smart used to mean being good at math and reading. No longer. Twenty years ago Howard Gardner, a cognitive psychologist at Harvard University, helped us both recognize and affirm what the church has claimed for two thousand years.

> We are not all the same; we do not all have the same kinds of minds. Taking human differences seriously lies at the heart of the MI [Multiple Intelligences] perspective.[1]

Sound familiar? It should. The Christian church's doctrine of humanity claims we are made in the image of God, every one unique, every one of value, every one gifted by God. How often have you said about children in your own church, "They are so different!" "They are all special." "They all have different gifts."? The message of the Christian church includes the understanding that taking human differences seriously lies at the heart of who we are as children of the living God.

When we consider uniqueness in relation to the human brain, we can connect with Gardner's theory of multiple intelligences. In this theory, Gardner proposes that humans are all unique; that uniqueness is brain-based; and that uniqueness deserves to be recognized. So, according to MI theory, instead of two ways of being intelligent, there are many ways in which humans are intelligent. Eight and one-half intelligences have been identified so far, and it is likely that more will be identified as we continue to learn more about the human brain and its incredible capacity for storing, retrieving, and processing information. In essence, multiple intelligences theory says, yes, there are math and reading intelligences (designated as linguistic and logical-mathematical intelligences in Gardner's theory), but there are other intelligences as well—intelligences we have neither recognized nor honored. We can be intelligent through:

- performing, creating, and appreciating musical patterns (musical intelligence)
- using our whole, and parts of, our bodies (bodily-kinesthetic intelligence)
- perceiving and manipulating objects and images in space (spatial intelligence)
- understanding and interacting with others (interpersonal intelligence)
- understanding and knowing ourselves (intrapersonal intelligence)
- recognizing and classifying the natural world (naturalist intelligence)
- exploring the nature of existence and related "big questions" (existential intelligence)

Additionally, Gardner proposes that all persons have all of the intelligences to some degree—a point that cannot be overemphasized for those who work with children.

What new definition of intelligence not only allows but demands this much broader and more comprehensive view of the ways in which persons are intelligent? When Gardner introduced his theory, he defined intelligence in this way: "An intelligence is the ability to solve problems, or to create products, that are valued within one or more cultural settings."[2] After years of monitoring pilot projects, observing the theory as it was translated into public education settings and responding to questions and reflections from educators, Gardner proposed a new definition: An intelligence is a "*biopsychological potential to process information* that can be activated in a cultural setting to solve problems or create products that are of value in a culture."[3] He explains, "This modest change in wording is important because it suggests that intelligences are not things that can be seen or counted. Instead, they are potentials—presumably neural ones—that will or will not be activated, depending upon the values of a particular culture, the opportunities available in that culture, and the personal decisions made by individuals and/or their families, schoolteachers, and others."[4]

There are some obvious implications of Gardner's understanding of intelligences for religious educators. First, North Americans value linguistic and logical-mathematical intelligences. We can count on our educational institutions to develop those intelligences to the point that makes them useful for teaching and learning the content we care about as religious educators. Therefore, we must engage those intelligences in our teaching/learning endeavors.

Second, the "others" in "personal decisions made by . . . others" in Gardner's definition includes religious educators. Religious educators have an opportunity to help children access their many intelligences and use them to process information that is life-giving and life-changing. That information, namely the gospel of Jesus Christ, deserves the opportunity to call on the abilities given us by God—brainpower, if you will—that can be defined in unique ways for each child. Religious educators have the power to make choices that influence the development of a variety of intelligences in children. It is our responsibility to see children in the fullness of their uniqueness and to design teaching activities that allow all children to bring their whole brains to the learning enterprise.

Third, this understanding of intelligence makes it clear that intelligence is not measured by how much a person knows but by the person's ability to work with information. It is a measure of knowing how to approach and figure out a problem, and how to learn a concept, how to use particular information that is available, and how to bring to a concept all the powers we have to more deeply understand it and be able to use it. Understanding the Bible and allowing it to shape our lives as disciples of Jesus Christ is a complicated task. It requires all our abilities and its attainment depends in part on a teacher's success in allowing all participants to call on those abilities. It also requires the recognition that the Holy Spirit is present in the teaching endeavor at least partly in this bestowal of varieties of gifts and abilities.

Each of the intelligences will be explored below, but first it is important to review the process by which Howard Gardner identified the intelligences he proposes. Many years of testing and research led

Gardner to posit eight criteria an intelligence must meet in order to be classified as such. The biological sciences, logical-mathematical analysis, developmental psychology, and traditional psychological research each contribute two criteria, covering everything from the locale of an intelligence in the brain to capacities that are central to an intelligence. Extensive descriptions of the criteria can be found in Gardner's first proposal of his theory in *Frames of Mind,* and the eight criteria are summarized in *Intelligence Reframed.*

One additional point about multiple intelligences theory is worth emphasizing. Intelligences do not operate alone. Rarely, if ever, do teaching/learning activities call upon one isolated intelligence. Brain locales house more than one intelligence. Activities that help learners enter the world of a concept call on more than one intelligence. Endeavors to truly understand a concept in depth likely utilize many intelligences. Developing an understanding of a concept results from engaging a number of intelligences and capitalizing on the multiple perspectives gained by going beyond the reliable but too narrow approach of seeing things solely through the lens of linguistic and logical-mathematical intelligences. These ideas will be explored later in this chapter in a discussion of the use of activities within teaching/learning settings.

Multiple Intelligences Theory: What It Isn't

As the theory of multiple intelligences has been advanced in the church, people have sometimes expressed confusion about how it differs from other previously popular theories or methods. Common responses to multiple intelligences theory include:

Sounds like learning styles to me. Learning styles came to be understood through educational theory and practice. The intelligences in Howard Gardner's MI theory are based on a psychological theory model. Each of the intelligences connect to a specific body of content. Learning styles or teaching models are used across bodies of subject matter, suggesting ways that persons prefer to learn any material.

It may be that individual learning styles influence how persons use their intelligences, but the two are not the same. For example, one person may usually choose to research information through print resources in a library or on the computer, while someone else may look for someone to ask. This represents a difference in learning styles, which in turn may lead to different aspects of an intelligence: the first person may enjoy listening to music, while the second may prefer to meet with one or two friends to create music.

Sounds like personality types to me. Many people who have taken personality tests of various types see similarities between the list of intelligences and the aspects of individual personalities. Intelligences do affect and influence personality. Preferred intelligences surely play an important role in the way persons interact with the world and with others.

Sounds like what we have always done in early childhood education. In a way, it is. The best teachers of young children (or any children, for that matter) have sought to involve as many senses of the children as possible. However, working with the MI theory is more than paying attention to the senses. Providing a time for the children to move around the room is just that—a break from sitting, not using the bodily-kinesthetic intelligence. To use bodily-kinesthetic intelligence would be to enter or explore a particular content to figure it out, such as learning sign language for an abstract word by beginning to define it with movement as well as words. While the names of some of the intelligences remind us of senses, such as linguistic or bodily-kinesthetic, no intelligence is dependent upon a single sense. For example, infants use their linguistic intelligence as they appropriate words and their meanings even before they can say the words. The spatial intelligence functions in persons without sight as well as persons who can see. The senses help us activate our intelligences, but intelligences are not limited to the senses and their capacity.

Sounds like a way to separate the children into groups. When applying MI theory to religious education for children, it is important to remember that every child has every one of these intelligences—and possibly many more. While there are preferred intelligences, each person can and needs to use each intelligence. As Christians, we might think of the intelligences as the gifts God has given to each child and the uniqueness of each child as the way that child uses the intelligences. If there is anything that needs to be guarded against in using MI theory in the church, it is using it to label and shortchange children in their potential.

A Brief Description of the Intelligences

(These descriptions may be photocopied for use in workshops)

The Linguistic Intelligence

Definition: The linguistic intelligence involves the heard, spoken, and written word and all the ways we use language.

What the Linguistic Intelligence Looks Like with Children

Linguistic intelligence begins with the babble of infants and progresses to understanding and speaking a language. As sounds become words and words become sentences, children are able to communicate with family members, church members, and persons in the community. The linguistic intelligence allows a person to communicate on many levels in both written and spoken language.

Skills Related to the Linguistic Intelligence

- convincing others, as in a debate
- remembering and recalling information (names, definitions, or lists), such as the books of the Bible
- explaining something, such as part of worship or how to find a Bible reference
- explaining its own activities, such as defining a theological term or writing a faith statement
- engaging in conversation for specific reasons, such as pursuing the meanings of a Bible story

Learning Activities That Engage the Linguistic Intelligence

- telling or hearing stories
- writing stories, poems, and letters
- discussing, debating, and interpreting information
- interviewing for information or opinion

The Logical-Mathematical Intelligence

Definition: The logical-mathematical intelligence is concerned with recognizing, identifying, and manipulating relationships and patterns. Symbols and numbers are often used to express these relationships and connections.

What the Logical-Mathematical Intelligence Looks Like with Children

While we tend to think first of mathematical applications, the logical-mathematical aspects of this intelligence are much more useful for religious education. Children using logical-mathematical intelligence often ask the "hard" questions of Bible stories. The logical-mathematical intelligence prompts children to experiment. They want to understand why things happen, and they like to figure out those "whys" for themselves. They use this intelligence to figure out reasons, draw conclusions, test possibilities, and describe why things happen the way they do. As patterns emerge, they can diagram connections and relationships.

Skills Related to the Logical-Mathematical Intelligence

- comparing ideas, such as the early church was like this, whereas our church is like this
- analyzing situations, such as selecting the main characters in the exodus story and examining their roles
- questioning causes, such as why all the disciples would run away when Jesus was arrested
- solving problems, such as why there are four Gospels and why they are different, or how the big bang theory and the two creation stories can all be "true"
- discovering relationships, such as how Paul interacted with the disciples, or how magic and miracle stories connected

Learning Activities That Engage the Logical-Mathematical Intelligence

- creating a time line
- posing open-ended problems
- providing information through coded material
- creating graphs to compare information

The Bodily-Kinesthetic Intelligence

Definition: Bodily-kinesthetic intelligence is best represented by the ability to use the whole body or parts of the body to demonstrate beauty, skill, planned movement, and purposeful action. It includes using parts of the body to manipulate objects.

What the Bodily-Kinesthetic Intelligence Looks Like with Children

Although we often think first of sports activities as representative of this intelligence, much more useful to Christian education is the expertise bodily-kinesthetic intelligence provides for interpreting meaning. Children utilizing bodily-kinesthetic intelligence use their bodies to represent stories, ideas, feelings, and action in movement through drama, dance, mime, gesture, role play, or facial expression.

They enjoy expressing their own interpretations, thoughts, ideas, and meanings in ways that use their fine motor and gross motor abilities.

Skills Related to the Bodily-Kinesthetic Intelligence

- representing story and emotion through acting
- using choreographed and spontaneous dance and creative body movement to tell and interpret
- manipulating objects and materials in order to create works of art and crafts, or participate in games and social activities
- using physical strength, agility, coordination, speed, flexibility, and endurance

Learning Activities That Engage the Bodily-Kinesthetic Intelligence

- dramatizing and role playing
- matching dance movements to words and/or music
- modeling clay or creating a God's eye
- teaching the meaning of concepts through sign language

The Spatial Intelligence

Definition: Spatial intelligence is concerned with seeing and understanding the relationships among objects and images in space. We use sculptures, drawings, pictures, graphics, designs, maps, and colors to represent these perceptions.

What the Spatial Intelligence Looks Like with Children

Although it may be tempting to believe the visual sense is always related to spatial intelligence, a person who is blind has spatial intelligence and can develop it, so the two are not always linked. Children using spatial intelligence create mental pictures of objects, relationships between objects, and action. They enjoy drawing, designing, illustrating, mapping, sculpting, creating models, and working with color. Their sense of direction is usually good, they like doing jigsaw puzzles, and they care about how things look on a page.

Skills Related to the Spatial Intelligence

- picturing in your mind what something represented in words looks like
- recognizing patterns and visual details
- making sense of landmarks, maps, charts, and diagrams
- constructing models and other kinds of visual representations of objects, scenes, and events
- manipulating color for effect

Learning Activities That Engage the Spatial Intelligence

- visualizing the scenes of a story
- creating a visual map of related ideas
- creating a computer-presented slide show
- constructing a model village

The Musical Intelligence

Definition: Musical intelligence gives us the capacity to recognize a sequence of musical sounds, from those of musical instruments to sounds of nature, and a sensitivity to rhythm and beat, from the rhythm of a dance band to the message sent in Morse code.

What the Musical Intelligence Looks Like with Children

The musical intelligence is the first to be observed in an infant, as the baby turns to the familiar tone of the mother's voice or waves arms and legs to the beat of music. This is usually followed by making tunes of one's own. As the musical intelligence is developed, a child uses it to enjoy music, to perform music, or to compose music, as well as to allow music in its many forms to affect his or her consciousness. The tie between the musical intelligence and emotion is so strong that it can soothe us in the hushed tone and gentle rhythm of a lullaby or excite us through the beat and energetic tone of a sports cheer.

Skills Related to the Musical Intelligence

- calming ourselves, as in a meditation
- producing sounds, as in making sound effects to accompany a dramatization of a Bible story
- memorizing, as in the names of the disciples set to music
- learning faith language, as in singing hymns
- creating rhythm patterns, as in telling a Bible story in rap or to a particular beat

Learning Activities That Engage the Musical Intelligence

- composing melodies
- preparing a choral reading
- accompanying a story with rhythm instruments
- listening to quiet music as prayer preparation

The Naturalist Intelligence

Definition: Naturalist intelligence involves the capacities to recognize and classify the many kinds of plants and animals in our world. Through the naturalist intelligence we come to an awareness of, and to care about, plants and animals as well as the environment.

What the Naturalist Intelligence Looks Like with Children

One need only observe a toddler intently watching a bug or caterpillar crawl along to realize that the observation of the natural world begins early. The way most kindergartners reel off the names of dinosaurs confirms the existence of the naturalist intelligence at an early age. Later on these capacities of observation, recognition, and classification can be applied to artificial things as well. Throughout life, the naturalist intelligence nurtures wonder and awe for the natural world and its order.

Skills Related to the Naturalist Intelligence

- recognizing members of a group, such as identifying what was created according to Genesis 1–2
- charting out the relationships among the parts of such, as practicing stewardship of God's creation
- recognizing differences within a group, such as seeing the importance of each part of the body
- demonstrating appreciation for all parts of the world, such as giving thanks and praise to God as Creator
- caring for living or growing things, such as planting bulbs

Learning Activities That Engage the Naturalist Intelligence

- planting seeds in different soils to understand the parable of the sower
- arranging a display of items from nature to encourage wonder
- collecting manufactured objects that help or hurt God's earth
- identifying likenesses and differences among children to affirm that uniqueness is good

The Interpersonal Intelligence

Definition: The interpersonal intelligence is concerned with one's ability to know, understand, and interact with other people. The capacity to make distinctions between people by "reading" their expressions, discerning what they are working toward, recognizing their moods, and understanding their point of view are all included in this intelligence.

What the Interpersonal Intelligence Looks Like with Children

Children using interpersonal intelligence distinguish easily among those around them, recognizing moods and desires, motivations and intentions. They enjoy learning in small groups, working on content with others rather than alone, discussing ideas, being part of a team, and sharing responsibility for processing and understanding information. They thrive in situations where working cooperatively is required or permitted, and their interpersonal skills bring leadership to a group trying to use their collective skills to process, interpret, and develop new ideas from information.

Skills Related to the Interpersonal Intelligence

- empathizing and sympathizing with others
- leading groups and planning with teams
- understanding others' thoughts, needs, and interpretations
- working with and caring for others
- communicating effectively with others

Learning Activities That Engage the Interpersonal Intelligence

- collaborating in a group to solve a problem
- working with others to plan and carry out a service project
- identifying a character's the feelings and motivations in a story
- paraphrasing the previous speaker in a discussion

The Intrapersonal Intelligence

Definition: The intrapersonal intelligence allows us to understand ourselves and to have access to our emotions. Through this intelligence, we develop self-esteem, self-image, and self-discipline.

What the Intrapersonal Intelligence Looks Like with Children

During the first three years of life, we go through a process of differentiating between ourselves and others. These boundaries are usually complete by age six. We continue to use the intrapersonal intelligence throughout our lives to understand abilities, behaviors, and emotions; to maintain an effective working model of ourselves; and to use that information to make decisions about our lives. As we separate our identity from others, we learn to trust, which is a necessary foundation for faith. Development of the intrapersonal intelligence is necessary for the development of the interpersonal intelligence.

Skills Related to the Intrapersonal Intelligence

- understanding our uniqueness, such as acknowledging our particular gifts from God
- seeing our mistakes, such as confessing to God
- enjoying ourselves, such as recognizing what brings us delight

- wondering about ourselves, such as pondering our purpose in this world
- reviewing our faith commitments, such as considering our stewardship

Learning Activities That Engage the Intrapersonal Intelligence

- writing a journal entry that describes feelings about a relationship
- identifying personal gifts for serving others
- praying a prayer of petition
- expressing personal values on a continuum

The Existential Intelligence

Definition: The existential intelligence gives us the capacity to see ourselves in relation to the breadth and depth of the universe and to ponder ourselves in relation to the most important and far-reaching questions of being human.

What the Existential Intelligence Looks Like with Children

Young children often astound us with their questions about the world around them and about such significant matters as life and death. While they may not be able to ponder these questions beyond their own experience, the questions are there. As they grow, the questions expand to cover more broadly the human condition, from the bad things that happen on the earth to the meaning of friendship. These questions invite them to explore the relationship of the Christian faith to our lives.

Skills Related to the Existential Intelligence

- coming to terms with loss, as when a grandparent dies
- engaging with the universe, as when we praise the Creator God
- thinking about goals, as when we encounter the call to discipleship
- seeing ourselves as part of the expanding universe, as when we encounter God in science
- exploring the nature of love, as in recognizing God's love for us

Learning Activities That Engage the Existential Intelligence

- inviting questions about who and whose we are
- considering the universe and God as creator of it
- presenting opportunities to serve and relating them to Jesus' call to discipleship

- asking "why" questions about stories, situations, and relationships

Increasing the Uses of Intelligences in Select Activities

Multiple intelligences theory is a wonderful tool for enriching ways we use common educational activities. With the list of intelligences in front of you, imagine enriching a simple activity by using it to engage intelligences in addition to those that are intrinsic to the activity itself. Let's look at six examples.

1. Make a collage
   Collect magazines, glue, scissors, markers, and a large piece of butcher paper or poster board. Direct the children to select words and pictures from the magazines that illustrate ways to praise God and reasons to praise God. Have them cut or tear them out and arrange them on the background so that they represent the theme "We praise God." (spatial, logical-mathematical)

   Ways to enrich the above activity by engaging other intelligences include:

   - As they work, ask each child individually how she or he most likes to praise God. (intrapersonal)
   - For part of the time, lead the children in a conversation about the parts of their own church's service that are praise centered. Encourage the children to work together to decide about less obvious elements, such as the sermon or hymns that are not obviously praise hymns. (logical-mathematical, interpersonal)
   - After all the pictures are selected but not yet glued to the paper, invite the children to group the pictures using the following categories, or other categories they determine: (interpersonal, logical-mathematical)

     - reasons to praise related to God's world
     - reasons to praise related to people as God's creation
     - reasons to praise related to music
     - reasons to praise related to use of our bodies
     - reasons to praise related to use of our minds

   - Invite a couple of children to watch the progress as pictures are selected. Have them select a hymn or two or a song they know that has similar ideas. They might write verses at appropriate places on the collage and prepare to lead the group in signing it. (musical)

- Lead a conversation around one big idea related to the collage theme, such as "Scientists continue to learn so many new things about the universe. How can God possibly be involved now in the natural world?" (existential)

2. Sing a song

Sing the well-known African American spiritual *Amen* to portray many of the stories about Jesus' life. (musical, linguistic)

Ways to enrich the above activity by engaging other intelligences include:

- Divide the verses among pairs or small groups of children. Have the children create simple hand and arm movements for each verse. (bodily-kinesthetic)
- Amen means "So be it," or "That's the way it is!" Have the children collectively decide on a movement that represents this idea to be used each time they sing the word "Amen." Emphasize refining the movement expression together. (bodily-kinesthetic, interpersonal)
- Assign each verse to a small group of children. Ask them to find in the gospels the stories represented in that verse, find out more about them, and be prepared to fill in the story with more details. (linguistic)
- Ask the children to consider the order of events in Jesus' life represented in the verses of the song. Are they in the same order as you would find the stories in the gospels? In all gospels? How would you reorder them? Why? (logical-mathematical)
- Provide one piece of poster board and a set of markers for each verse. Assign a verse to small groups of children and ask them to illustrate one story from their verse. (spatial)
- Provide pictures of events in Jesus' life. Ask the children to match as many pictures as they can to stories referred to in the song. (spatial, logical-mathematical)

3. Create a drama

Form three groups. Give each group one of three scenes from the time just before Jesus' crucifixion: the garden of Gethsemane, the courtyard of the High Priest where Peter denied Jesus, or preparation for the crucifixion and the road to Golgotha. Invite each group to create a dramatization of its scene. (bodily-kinesthetic, spatial, linguistic)

Ways to enrich the above activity by engaging other intelligences include:

- Ask each group to select a song, verse, or background music that goes with its scene. (musical, logical-mathematical)
- Ask members of each group to talk together about their scene, and to choose one hard question about God that arises from it. Explain that a hard question is a question with no one right answer, one that invites lots of ideas and possibilities and is often an "I wonder" question. The small group might direct its question to the whole group at the end of the dramatization of their scene. (existential)
- Ask the children to imagine the sights, smells, and sounds around them in their scene. (All scenes are outdoors.) Invite them to select something that could be significant for the story from the surroundings in their scene and to represent it in their drama. (naturalist)
- Invite the group to decide on the most important parts of the scene. Ask the children to illustrate the key feelings/actions in one or two tableaux from the scene, using their face and their entire body to illustrate them. (interpersonal, bodily-kinesthetic)
- Ask the children to take time in quiet before planning the drama to imagine what they would be feeling if they were Jesus. Use these questions to guide their thinking: What just happened to you (Jesus) in the time before this scene? How does that leave you feeling? What is happening now? What are you feeling now? (intrapersonal)

4. Teach with pictures

   Provide twenty pictures that represent key stories from the Old Testament, together with references for where the stories can be found in the Bible. Invite the children to select a story they don't know much about, look it up, read it, and be prepared to tell it to someone else, using the picture to help them. (spatial, linguistic)

Ways to enrich the above activity by engaging other intelligences include:

- Once they have read the story, invite the children to paint a picture that represents something important in the story, other than the action represented in the picture they have in hand. (spatial, linguistic, logical-mathematical)
- Provide musical/rhythm instruments and invite the children to select one and play it during a part of their story to heighten the action. (musical)
- Ask participants to read the story, watching for the part of the story that is the turning point, or the key action. Invite them to work with a partner to demonstrate this important moment with their bodies, with just their faces, and with their movements in a way designed to help others see and understand its importance. (bodily-kinesthetic, interpersonal)
- Ask children to spend five minutes looking closely at their pictures before they read the story, using either their own wondering to guide reflection or the following questions (intrapersonal):

    a. Look for what is happening in the setting and surroundings. What might have come before this scene? What might come after it?
    b. Focus on one character in the picture. What is that person doing? What is happening to that person? What might be going through that person's mind? What is that person feeling?
    c. What might the picture be saying to you?

- Invite the children to imagine together, in pairs or groups of three, what story this picture tells. Then decide together on at least five questions based on the picture that they would like to have answers for, and invite them to look for the answers when they read the story. (interpersonal, logical-mathematical)

5. Tell a story

   Tell the story of the Good Samaritan to the children. (linguistic)

   Ways to enrich the activity by engaging other intelligences:

   - Form three groups. Give each group a separate character with which to identify. Ask them to imagine while they listen that they are the Samaritan, the priest, or the Levite and to wonder why they are making the choices they make. (logical-mathematical, intrapersonal)

- As they listen to the story, invite the children to close their eyes and create mental pictures of the action as it unfolds. Tell them to pay attention to their impression of the scene and the characters so they can describe to the whole group what they picture. (spatial, linguistic)

- As they listen, invite the children to pay particular attention to the actions of the characters in the story. Tell them if they close their eyes and imagine seeing the story as a video, they might be able to hear background music that highlights the action. Ask them to be ready to tell the group what songs came to mind as they heard the story. (linguistic, spatial, musical)

- Provide each set of two or three participants with a chart with two columns, identified as "Reasons to stop and help" and "Reasons to pass by," and a list of the characters from the story printed down the left side. Provide a description of each character's position ("job" position and position in society). Ask the children, after hearing the story, to list for each person good reasons to stop and help and good reasons to pass by. Invite them to talk with members of their group and write down only the reasons on which they all agree. (linguistic, logical-mathematical, interpersonal)

- Explain that the questioner asks Jesus, "Who is my neighbor?" and Jesus tells this story. Most people think Jesus will answer that question with the story and the answer will be, "My neighbor is anyone who needs help, in this case the man who is beaten and robbed." But Jesus turns the question around and instead asks the questioner who was the neighbor of the man in need. The neighbor then becomes the one who acts on behalf of others. Provide newspapers and news magazines. Ask the children to find stories about people, groups, or countries who act on behalf of others. In small groups, have them tell the stories they find and talk about what kind of people work for others and what motivates people to do what they do for others. Use what the small groups have learned to lead a whole group discussion of the questions, "Who is Jesus?" and

"What does Jesus expect of us?" (existential, interpersonal, logical-mathematical, linguistic)

6. Lead a discussion or conversation
   After telling the story of the lost sheep, use these questions to lead a conversation about the story:

   a. Why is the shepherd worried about the sheep?
   b. Would you be more concerned about keeping ninety-nine safe or searching for the lost one?
   c. What do we know about the work of shepherds in Jesus' time?
   d. How does what we know help us understand this story?
   e. Jesus used the story to tell us what God is like. What did you learn from this story about what God is like? (linguistic, logical-mathematical)

Ways to enrich the above activity with questions that engage children's many intelligences include:

- Discuss these questions: What do you think God is like? Why might we all have different ideas about what God is like? What do you think people of other faiths, such as Jews, Hindus, or Muslims, might think God is like? (existential)

- Say to the children, "Now that we have talked about the story, what questions do you have?" List their questions on newsprint. Provide Bible dictionaries, articles about the land of Israel at the time of Jesus and different occupations, children's Bible concordances, and various Bible translations for children, and ask the group to find answers for their questions. (logical-mathematical, linguistic)

- Invite the children to find a place by themselves and think about these questions: What does it feel like to be lost or alone? Does it help to know someone is looking for you? Why? Think about people you know at school. Do you know anyone who seems lost or alone? What makes you think that? Children can be lost by being separated from family members. In what other situations might a child feel lost? (intrapersonal)

- Invite the children to close their eyes. Use questions and directions like the following to help them meditate on being lost and being loved: *Remember a time you lost something important to you. What was it? Picture it in your mind. How did you feel when you didn't think you could find it? Is it still lost? If it is still lost, what are you thinking about it right now? If you found it, how did that make you feel? Now imagine someone very important to you, someone you want never to be without. Imagine that person loving you, hugging you. Imagine you hugging and loving that person. What does it feel like? Imagine God loving you that much. Imagine God wanting you close all the time. Imagine that God will always look out for you no matter what.* (intrapersonal)

- Ask the children to think about the way movies use music to help people get involved in the stories they are telling. Ask them what kind of music goes with the feelings of being lost, scared, left alone, caught in a trap of some kind, and not included in a group. Ask what lines from songs or hymns come to mind when they think about being lost and God's love that won't let us go. (musical)

Workshops

Applying the theory of multiple intelligences to ministry with children can help leaders see each child as unique—a special creation of God. It can also help leaders nurture each child to be a faithful disciple of Jesus Christ, contributing through their unique gifts. Two workshops designed to help leaders understand and use multiple intelligence theory with children in your congregation are outlined below. The first provides introduction to the MI theory and allows participants to experience some aspects of each intelligence. The second workshop focuses on adjusting session plans that are currently in use to include additional intelligences.

A Workshop to Introduce the Multiple Intelligences Theory

Purpose: To introduce teachers to the theory of multiple intelligences.
Time: 1½–2 hours

Materials:
Copies of the brief description of each intelligence (pp. 56–62)
Nine gift bags
Writing paper and pencils
Drawing paper and crayons
Modeling clay
Newsprint and markers
Bibles or nine copies of Luke 9:20–27
Nine tables/sites

Opening prayer: Holy Giver of Gifts, open us to your Spirit that we may discover your gifts within us and use those gifts and the knowledge we gain here to equip the saints of all ages for your ministry. Amen.

Block A (about 10 minutes): Presentation on definition of intelligences (what they are and what they are not), see pages 56–62.

Block B (50–60 minutes): Multiple Intelligences Centers
Preparation: Review the description of the Multiple Intelligences Centers below. Prepare and place the directions and materials in gift bags and put one bag per type of intelligence at each table.
Step 1: Divide the participants into nine groups and invite each group to sit at a table.
Step 2: Read the story from Luke 9:10–17.
Step 3: Have the groups proceed with the activities on their tables.

Step 4: After five minutes, ask the groups to put everything back the way they found it and rotate clockwise to the next table. Continue rotation every five minutes until each group has had a chance to work at each table.

Step 5: Have the participants each take a moment to discuss with a partner what they learned from this experience about themselves or about how people learn.

Block C (about 20–30 minutes): Review the definition of intelligence that Gardner uses and briefly describe each intelligence. Allow some time for questions and discussion. Conclude with a statement like, In 1 Corinthians 12, Paul talks about the great variety of gifts of the Spirit. Intelligences are like those gifts, and each person is gifted by God to use the intelligences in different ways, which makes each person unique. We in the church must surely recognize the uniqueness of each person, and the theory of multiple intelligences provides another way for us to remember that as we plan and teach God's Word.

Closing prayer: God of all life, thank you for all our intelligences and the uniqueness of each of us. Send us on our way filled with the knowledge of your presence and your love, so that we might show that love through all that we do and say. In Jesus' name, Amen.

Directions of Centers for Block B

Have Bibles on hand for the participants to review the story in Luke 9:10–17 or have copies of the passage for each center.

Linguistic Intelligence: (writing paper, pencils)

Discuss this question within your group: What does the story in Luke 9:10–17 say to Christians in the twenty-first century? Or ask the children to pretend they are one of the five thousand men. Write a letter to a friend telling what you saw and did.

Logical-Mathematical Intelligence: (writing paper, pencils)

Luke reports that there were five thousand men present. If they sat down in groups of fifty each, how many groups would that be? If there were five loaves of bread, how much bread did each group receive? Or talk together about ways to distribute the food to the groups. Look for the pros and cons of each plan.

Bodily-Kinesthetic Intelligence:

As a group or individually, mime the story of the feeding of the five thousand. Do it at least three times, adding more detail each time. Remember, no talking when miming. Or act out the story together. Everyone should have a part. Then act it out again, adding more interaction among the people than is found in the text.

Spatial Intelligence: (drawing paper, crayons, modeling clay)

See the story in your imagination. Watch the characters move through the action of verse 10 through verse 17. Describe to the group the most vivid scene that you imagined. Or use the art supplies to create a picture or a symbol of the story from Luke.

Musical Intelligence: (newsprint, markers)

Write a song about this story to the tune of "'Are You Sleeping?" Sing it together. Or create sound effects for the story, and have one person read it as the rest of the group provides the sound effects.

Naturalist Intelligence:

Luke gives no details about the setting for the story, except that it is removed from the village of Bethsaida. Describe what you think the setting and scenery are for the feeding of the five thousand. Include smells, sounds, textures that you might feel, as well as what you might see. Or imagine you are to tell this story during worship for the time with children. You want the children to enter into the story as fully as possible. List images based on the five senses that will make the story alive for them.

Interpersonal Intelligence:

Pretend you are the disciples and you are sitting around those twelve baskets of broken pieces of bread. Have a conversation about what you saw. Remember you have just returned from a trip on which you spread the good news and cured diseases (see Luke 9:1–6). Or imagine you are a committee that is to develop plans for introducing a new food pantry at an intergenerational event in your church. Together you have just read Luke 9:10–17. Begin your planning.

Intrapersonal Intelligence: (writing paper, pencils)

Use this story as a means of meditation. Read the story silently, and when you come to an image or group of words that grabs you, stop and meditate on that image or those words. Or pray or write a prayer of confession prompted by reading this story.

Existential Intelligence:

Think about this story and ponder this question: How does this story call me to discipleship in Jesus Christ? Or discuss together answers for the eight-year-old child, who asks, "Is this story real?"

A Workshop for Enriching Session Plans

Purpose: To provide teachers with a process for enriching a session plan by adding or substituting activities that engage additional or alternate intelligences.

Time: 1½–2 hours

Materials

Copies of the brief description of each intelligence (pp. 56–62)

Activity cards (prepare ahead of time based on pp. 75–76)

Copies of the printed instructions and list of intelligences (p. 77)

Teacher's guides and children's materials

Eight sheets of blank paper and markers for each small group

Signs for each intelligence

Newsprint

Ten tables/sites

Opening prayer: God of all people, you have made us unique creatures, with different gifts and skills and interests and intelligences. Help us as teachers to recognize the diversity in the children you have called us to teach and to nurture each one as your child. Remind us that your church survives and thrives because its head is your son, Jesus Christ, in whose name we pray. Amen.

Block A (about 15 minutes)

Preparation: Set up nine tables, each with multiple copies of the definition sheet for one intelligence. Prepare a table with stacks of activity cards (each containing a one-sentence description of an activity that primarily engages that intelligence) for each intelligence. Place a sign identifying the intelligence next to each stack.

Step 1: Take three cards per participant for the stacks. Shuffle the cards and distribute three to each participant.

Step 2: Instruct participants as follows: visit each table, taking a copy of the description of each intelligence; determine which intelligences the activities on your cards primarily engage; leave each card on the appropriate table; work in pairs to determine the intelligences engaged; remember that the activities will often engage more than one intelligence.

Step 3: After ten minutes, ask participants to collect the cards from each table and place them beside the appropriate sign on the activity cards table.

Block B (about 30–40 minutes)

Divide participants into groups of five or six, preferably by grouping teachers who teach similar age levels or who use the same teacher resources. Provide each participant with a copy of the printed instructions and intelligences list.

Block C (about 10 minutes per group)

Invite each group to stand in a line with their session activities in order and report. Encourage the other groups to ask questions and to suggest alternative orders by moving the people in the line. The following questions may encourage creativity:

- If we removed this (select an activity) activity, what other activity representing another intelligence might we replace it with?
- Suggest an activity for this place that engages the [select an intelligence] intelligence.
- If we removed this (select an activity) activity, what other intelligence might we engage here that is not represented?

At the end of each group's presentation, ask the whole group, "What other changes might we make to help ensure that this session plan builds understanding of the story or concept presented?"

Block D (10 minutes) Lead the group in a discussion of the steps they took to revise their session plans to develop a process for enriching session plans.

Closing prayer: We thank you, O God, for making us in your image, a reflection of your creative and shaping and guiding Spirit. May we use our energies, which are also a gift from you, to more creatively shape and guide the children entrusted to our care. Amen.

Items for Activity Cards

Linguistic Intelligence

Write a journal entry

Select words from a hymn that illustrate an idea

Tell a story

Listen to a story

Write five questions you have about a concept or story

Use the print resources to answer questions about a concept or story

Write a haiku poem that illustrates a story or concept

With two other people write a one-page dramatization of a story

Write a letter to a friend about what you have learned

Interview another person in the group about his or her view of a concept or story

Logical-Mathematical Intelligence

Select from magazines words and pictures that illustrate a story or concept

Sort pictures into groups that illustrate the feelings and/or actions of characters in a story

Compare the responses of two characters in a story

Think of the words of at least three songs that relate to a story or concept

Decide on the two most important actions taken in a story and tell a partner why you think they are important

Make a chart that has all the characters in a story down one side and all the major feelings represented in the story across the top. Use a check mark in the boxes to indicate which characters had each feeling

List three reasons why something happened

Create a time line of the action in a story

Solve an open-ended problem related to a story or concept

Examine the role of the main character in a story and consider how that person might have acted differently

Musical Intelligence

Write a simple tune that brings out a concept or story line

Select a rhythm instrument and plan how to use it to help tell a story

Sing a song that tells a story

Participate in a choral reading of a dramatization of a story

Listen to quiet, meditative music to prepare to hear a story

Write a rap of a story, using the rhythmic pattern to convey the meaning

Use a drum beat to add emphasis to a story

Select instrumental lines from popular music to express the different moods of a story

Tap your feet and/or clap your hands to highlight the action of a story

Write a short, rhythmic chant to insert into the telling of a story to highlight the action

Bodily-Kinesthetic Intelligence

Show facial expressions that express the successive moods of a story

Tell a story in mime

Dramatize a story

Create a puppet show to tell a story

Plan dance movements that express the action of a story

Use your hands to create a craft related to a story

Play a game of charades using key words or actions from a story

Role-play possible endings for a story

Create a sculpture of a character in a story

Learn to tell a story in sign language

Spatial Intelligence

Draw a picture to show the action of a scene in a story

Combine visual images cut from magazines to represent a mood or feeling from a story

Use colored chalk on wet construction paper to represent an event from a story

Close your eyes and visualize the successive scenes in a story

Construct a model of a scene in a story

Picture in your mind the visual features of a setting

Draw a cartoon that illustrates the scenes of a story

Create a set for dramatization of a story

Create a relief map of a place

Work on a jigsaw puzzle picture of a story scene

Interpersonal Intelligence

Solve a problem in cooperation with others

Work with others to create a time line or model or relief map

Teach others a story you have just learned

Create a role play in which you let another person know you have understood what they said

Work as a group to resolve a situation of conflict

Imagine another person's feelings and response in a situation

Work as a team to decipher a code or puzzle

Identify the feelings and motivations of a character in a story

Work with a group on a service project

Describe all the needs of the characters in a story

Intrapersonal Intelligence

Participate in a guided mediation

Write a prayer of personal confession

Write a journal entry about your response to a story

Describe how you would have responded in a particular situation

Tell someone about your gifts

Wonder about what God is calling you to do

Express your opinion about an ethical situation

Sculpt a symbol of an image you have of God

Sit alone and think about what you hope for your life

Read a poem and ponder its meaning for you

Naturalist Intelligence

Take a walk in a natural setting, looking for things you imagine in a story

Relate patterns of symmetry or asymmetry in nature to a story

Consider relationships between the natural world and what humans have created

Pray a prayer of thanks for things you name that God has created

Plant seeds and watch their growth

Collect things that show the world around us

Identify similarities and differences among people

Create a display of things from nature that symbolize new life

Wonder about how God made all the natural wonders of the world

Discover how a part of the body functions in relation to other parts

Existential Intelligence

Wonder about who we are in relation to God

Read a psalm about creation and imagine the amazing diversity of the world

Visit a funeral home and talk with others about what happens when we die

Write a journal entry about what it means to love God

Consider what God might be calling you to do with your life

Pick one way to serve God by serving others

Read a story about relationships and talk with others about how we are connected to each other

Write down questions you have about the world and our existence

Ask people you trust to tell you what they believe about Jesus

Think of one bad thing that happened to a friend and why it might have happened

Printed instructions and intelligences list

1. Using a session plan from your teacher materials (or one provided by the workshop leader), review all of the activities for that session and note which intelligence(s) the activity engages.
2. Using this list of the nine intelligences, circle the ones the session plan does not use:

Linguistic

Logical-Mathematical

Musical

Bodily-Kinesthetic

Spatial

Interpersonal

Intrapersonal

Naturalist

Existential

3. Select two or three intelligences for which you will add activities to the session plan, or use to exchange for intelligences that are overused in the plan. If the plan already engages a variety of intelligences, select two or three intelligences to utilize in substitute activities, because you believe they would better serve the session or better serve a particular group of children, or for the purposes of practicing the skill of selecting intelligences and enriching session plans.
4. Using your own ideas of activities, or activity cards you select from the table, agree upon two or three activities that enrich the session plan. Determine how the activity will be presented and where it will be inserted in the session plan.
5. Discuss the following questions in your small group:
   - How many different intelligences does the revised plan now engage?
   - Do the relationship and order of the activities help provide the diversity the session plan needs? Why or why not?
6. Put the activities of your revised session plan in numbered order on the blank sheets of paper provided. Be prepared to stand in a row, holding the sheets with the listed activities in order, and briefly describe to the whole group what you took out, what you put in, and why.

NOTES

1. Gardner, Howard C., *Intelligence Reframed* (New York: Basic Books, 1999) 91.
2. Gardner, Howard C., *Frames of Mind: The Theory of Multiple Intelligences* (New York: Basic Books, 1983) x.
3. *Intelligence Reframed*, 33–4, emphasis added.
4. *Intelligence Reframed*, 34.

RESOURCES

A Sampling of Books by Howard Gardner

Frames of Mind: The Theory of Multiple Intelligences. New York: Basic Books, 1983.

The Unschooled Mind: How Children Think and How Schools Should Teach. New York: Basic Books, 1993.

Leading Minds: An Anatomy of Leadership. New York: Basic Books, 1996.

Extraordinary Minds: Portrait of Exceptional Individuals and an Examination of Our Extraordinariness. New York: Basic Books, 1997.

Intelligence Reframed: Multiple Intelligences for the 21st Century. New York: Basic Books, 1999.

The Disciplined Mind: Beyond Facts and Standardized Tests, The K-12 Education That Every Child Deserves. New York: Simon & Schuster, 2000.

Books about and Using MI Theory

Armstrong, Thomas. *Multiple Intelligences in the Classroom.* (2nd ed.) Alexandria, VA: Association for Supervision and Curriculum Development, 2001.

_____. *In Their Own Way.* New York: Tarcher/Putnam, 1987.

Kagan, Spencer, and Miguel Kagan. *Multiple Intelligences: The Complete MI Book.* San Clemente, CA: Kagan Cooperative Learning, 1998.

Lazear, David. *Eight Ways of Knowing.* Arlington Heights, IL: IRI/Skylight Publishing, 1991.

_____. *Eight Ways of Teaching.* Arlington Heights, IL: IRI/Skylight Publishing, 1991.

_____. *Eight Pathways of Learning.* Tucson, AR: Zephyr Press, 1999.

CHAPTER FOUR

Welcoming Children and Removing Stumbling Blocks: The Church's Child Advocacy Ministry

Rebecca L. Davis

He was four years old when he invited the adults who regularly assembled in the fellowship hall into a new understanding of themselves and their world. With his black hair cut close to his head, sky-blue eyes, and a smattering of freckles, Jason bounded off the bus each afternoon for the after-school program. Jason was a charmer, a quiet child who rarely used words, but whose smile lit up the room around him. No one could resist Jason when he put the full force of his gifts behind a request, but requests were infrequent. Jason accepted what came his way with grace and a sense of dignity that was well beyond his years.

Jason was among the fifty children between the ages of four and ten who were dropped off at the small Presbyterian church for afternoons of tutoring, recreation, art, music, enrichment programs, and a hearty snack. The church after-school program served children whose parents worked at jobs that did not afford the luxury of quality child-care. Instead of being home alone, these children benefited from adult nurture, homework help, enrichment programs, and safe surroundings.

It was October when a pattern was brought to the attention of the pastor. Every afternoon Jason would eat exactly one-half of his snack and place the remainder in his backpack. With careful precision he divided his food, savored one half, then wrapped and tucked away the second half. When the caregivers offered Jason more, he smiled and asked to be excused to play until the others finished. When asked if he wanted to finish his snack, he would simply say, "No." After several weeks, the adults questioned the one person who could be counted on to speak for Jason—his sister Emily.

Emily, a six-year-old veteran of the after-school program, was as talkative as Jason was reticent. Emily's matter-of-fact response was that Jason was smarter than she because he saved half his food so he would have something to eat for dinner—unless their mom needed to eat it before she went to work. As she finished her explanation and happily skipped off to the swing set, the caregivers fought to catch their breath and blink back tears. In the words of a six-year-old and the actions of a four-year-old, their understanding of the world was changed forever.

What is wrong with a world where four-year-olds have to carefully ration their snacks so that the hours before bedtime are not spent in gnawing hunger? What is wrong with a world that forms children with such low expectations that they refuse to ask for more food and speak matter-of-factly of harsh realities? What is wrong with a world when a mother has to choose between food for her children and a place for them to sleep? And what are we the church called to do about it?

Emily's explanation provided a disorienting dilemma for her care-givers that day. No longer could they live blissfully unaware of the circumstances that are a daily reality for too many children and families. Never again would they be able to hear the words of Matt. 25:44, "Lord when was it that we saw you hungry or thirsty or naked . . . and did not take care of you?" without seeing Jason dividing his snack. This was the day many of these ordinary, faithful people began their journeys of becoming child advocates. They were propelled into action to help Jason's family find the community resources and education they needed to begin the long, slow climb out of extreme poverty. They also began their own education, learning how difficult and frustrating it can be to work within societal structures to make a difference and how challenging it can be to be faithful to the call of Jesus on behalf of the poor.

Defining Child Advocacy

According to Matthew 18, when the disciples asked Jesus who was the greatest in the kingdom of heaven, Jesus responded by calling a child into their midst and saying,

> Truly I tell you, unless you change and become like children, you will never enter the kingdom of heaven. Whoever becomes humble like this child is the greatest in the kingdom of heaven. Whoever

welcomes one such child in my name welcomes me. If any of you put a stumbling block before one of these little ones who believe in me, it would be better for you if a great millstone were fastened around your neck and you were drowned in the depth of the sea. Woe to the world because of stumbling blocks! Occasions for stumbling are bound to come, but woe to the one by whom the stumbling block comes! (Matt. 18: 3-6)

In this explicit and emphatic commission, Jesus provides a foundational definition of child advocacy—welcome children and remove stumbling blocks.

Welcoming Children

In the ancient Near Eastern culture, welcoming children was a radical concept. Children were viewed as property and were without rights in the society. Within the Jewish tradition, however, was evidence of an alternative voice that promoted the value of children. From Genesis, where all human beings (not just adult human beings) are declared to be created in the image of God to the Midrash, where children are seen as good guarantors to whom the Torah is given, theological arguments are found that champion children and their inherent value. Jesus reinforced and expanded this tradition when he commanded his disciples to welcome children. According to the version of the story as it is found in the Gospel of Mark (9:33–37), Jesus proclaims that when we welcome a child we welcome Jesus himself and the One who sent him. Who among us would dare not welcome Christ or the Sovereign God of the Universe?

Welcome the little children, Jesus commands. What is the nature of that welcome? The welcome of Jesus is the welcome that comes from and in the name of the one who proclaimed, "The Spirit of the Lord is upon me, because he has anointed me to bring good news to the poor. He has sent me to proclaim release to the captives and recovery of sight to the blind, to let the oppressed go free, to proclaim the year of the Lord's favor" (Luke 4:18–19). The welcome that we are commanded to give to children is one that transforms lives, uplifts the poor, offers healing, and sets people free.

Removing Stumbling Blocks

As recorded in Matt. 18:6–7, Jesus' words are clear, his tone imperative, and the consequences of causing children to stumble explicit. Stumbling blocks are a reality, but if we are the cause, it would be better that a great millstone be fastened around our necks and we be drowned in the sea. Stumbling blocks come in many forms for children in contemporary society. For some, the lack of affordable, quality child care or lack of adequate preparation will cause them to stumble as they enter school. For others, it will be the lack of health insurance or the experience of ridicule for not meeting social norms of style, scholastic aptitude, or morality. Whatever interferes with a child's ability to live into the fullness for which God created him or her is a stumbling block.

The predominant message given to our children in our society is that they are acceptable only if they buy this item, wear that brand, have a particular car, and look or act a certain way. This message is counter to the message of the Gospel that says all are valuable, worthy, lovable, and acceptable because they are God's own. This is the message that the church is called to bring to children in a ministry of child advocacy—a ministry of welcoming children and removing stumbling blocks from their way. When members of the Presbyterian church that hosted Jason's after-school program began living out this calling, some significant questions arose within the congregation. Since Jason and his family were not involved in the church, some wondered why it was the church's business to take care of them. Other questions followed—Who? Where? How? When?—questions most of us will have to address as we begin our journey of becoming child advocates.

The Why of Child Advocacy

The Image of God

Robert and his wife were retired and enjoying spending time on things that added meaning and pleasure to their lives. Both were active in church and in their social circles. Robert had a passion for adult education and mission. He was active in the presbytery and in Habitat for Humanity. One day during church school he told about one of his most memorable experiences working with Habitat. Describing himself as not particularly child-friendly, Robert was on the roof of a house under construction one hot summer day. A young Latino volunteer wanted desperately to help out. Robert did everything he could do, politely and sometimes not so politely, to discourage the young man. As it often is with the young their tenacity outdistances their age and Robert finally gave in grudgingly. He offered to let the boy hand him nails, which Robert hammered into the roof. The heat rose, and the day wore on, and the duo continued to work side by side. Robert realized that the work was going faster and smoother with his helper and gruffly said to the young man, "Well son, if we're going to be partners and work together, we might as well know one another's name. I'm Robert." To which the young man replied, extending his hand, "I'm Jesus."

It is not often that we are so bluntly reminded that each person is created in the image of God. If we say take seriously what Genesis teaches, "Then God said, 'Let us make humankind in our image, according to our likeness,'" we believe that within every human, within every child, lies the very image of God. This reality makes us kin with one another, connecting us in an inviolate relationship. In his book *Love and Conflict: A Covenantal Model of Christian Ethics*, Joseph Allen suggests that humans are connected by an inclusive covenant with God and one another by virtue of our relatedness to and creation by God.[1] When we look into the faces of our brothers and sisters, our neighbors, our mothers, our enemies, our children, we see our own kin and the very image of God. How well are we tending the image of God? Whenever children go to sleep hungry, know the feeling of fist connecting with flesh, or are taught that they are unworthy and unequal because of the color of their skin or the station of their birth, we are neglecting the sacred trust of God's image and our kin.

The Covenant of Baptism

One of the primary identities of Christians is that of being a covenant people. Entering into a covenant requires a mutual and reciprocal act of entrustment. Entrustment occurs when parties give to one another something of value, trusting that the gift will be honored, treasured, and well cared for by the other. In the giving and receiving, a new moral (moral meaning ethical rather than virtuous) community is formed, in which participants are bound together in a life-defining way.[2] Members of the covenant community are responsible to and for one another, knit together in mutual accountability. Covenants are also enduring and, according to Allen, take two forms: inclusive covenants and special covenants.[3] Inclusive covenants are initiated by God, who determines the parameters. God is also central in special covenants and human beings intentionally enter into the relationship, which is characterized by a set of rules that apply to those who participate in it. Marriage is an example of a special covenant.

The baptism of children seals a special covenant through which participants—God, parents or guardians, children, congregations, and the church universal—enter into a moral community. Sacred vows are taken in which adult participants promise to care for children, to be partners in their parenting, to show them the love, grace, and mercy of God, and to teach them that their identity as members of the household of faith is their primary identity and one that obliterates the destructive messages of the world. In each baptismal service, we become responsible for all the participants of the covenant. We renew our own baptismal vows, and with them, our life-long commitment to ministry and discipleship. Baptism issues its own call to child advocacy and compels us to ask "Are we keeping our vows?" and "Where is the integrity of our faith if we do not keep our baptismal promises through advocacy for children?"

Children who live with violence in their neighborhoods and schools will have a difficult time coming to know and trust in a Prince of Peace. Little ones who suffer abuse and neglect are likely to distrust adults and disbelieve assurances, blessed or otherwise. The world we live in and what happens to children in this world is directly related to our baptismal covenant, but what of children who are not baptized? The promises of baptism are not just in effect within the church walls and for children whose names we know. In baptism we are not only receivers of grace; we are also ordained into a lifetime of service and ministry, continuing Jesus' ministry until he returns. Baptism propels us into transformational ministry on behalf of all children because the way of Christ is liberating, healing, comforting, just, and inclusive. When Peter responded in the affirmative to Jesus' question, "Do you love me?," Jesus admonished him, "Feed my lambs" (John 21:15). The vows of baptism are our affirmative response to the question from Jesus, "Do you love me?," and the whole of creation is the sphere in which we validate that response by feeding his lambs.

Practical Considerations

Faithfulness may not always be practical, yet part of the task of advocating for children is to encourage others, including those who may not feel compelled by faith, to accept this responsibility as well. One way to approach this is to be clear on the practical consequences of working on behalf of children. Child advocacy is a wise investment. Consider the following information compiled by the Children's Defense Fund in Washington, DC. Every dollar spent:

- vaccinating children against measles, mumps, and rubella will save $16 in medical costs to treat those illnesses later

- for the Supplemental Food Program for Women, Infants, and Children (WIC) saves $3 in future costs
- on quality early childhood care and education saves $7 by increasing the likelihood that children will be literate, employed, and enrolled in postsecondary education and less likely to be school dropouts, dependent on welfare, or arrested for criminal activity[4]

The Who of Child Advocacy

"Perhaps we cannot prevent this world from being a world in which children are tortured. But we can reduce the number of tortured children. And if you [believers] don't help us, who else in the world can help us do this?"[5] Who will be advocates for children? The challenge of Albert Camus in the quote above and the directives of our faith say that we, as individual believers and as the church, are to fulfill this role. The task of child advocacy is both a corporate and an individual task. Every person of faith is called to be a child advocate. Pastors, educators, church school teachers, elders, deacons, choristers, church women, men, youth, and adults all have the responsibility and the privilege of joining their voices and witnessing for children. Those ordinary people of faith who helped Jason did not necessarily define themselves as child advocates, and when they stopped to think after the initial flurry of activities, they were more than a little uneasy. They need not have worried. They were not the first to be anxious at the realization of a new way of being a disciple.

According to the Gospel of John, when Jesus gathered his disciples on that evening before the festival of Passover, he washed their feet and unsettled their minds. He told them that change was about to happen. He would be leaving them. The disciples panicked. Who would they be without Jesus to follow? How would they carry on after he was gone? In response, Jesus first set his expectations clearly before them.

> For I have set you an example, that you also should do as I have done to you love one another. Just as I have loved you, you also should love one another. By this, everyone will know that you are my disciples (John 13:15, 34–35).

Jesus tells his followers to do as he has done. How in the world were those disciples, those ordinary people going to do that extraordinary work? Jesus continues with a promise:

> I will ask the Father, and he will give you another advocate, to be
> with you forever. He abides with you and he will be in you have said
> these things to you while I am still with you. But the advocate, the
> Holy Spirit, whom the Father will send in my name, will teach you
> everything, and remind you of all that I have said to you (John
> 14:16–17, 26).

The Greek word *parakletos*, translated here as "advocate," is
used exclusively in the Johannine writings. It literally means "called
to one's aid" and is translated variously as helper, comforter, spirit,
and advocate. The word connotes summoned in aid, beseeching, or
evoking divine help, speaking on behalf of, encouraging, and comforting in sorrow or difficulty. The gifts of the advocate who abides in
believers are the tools of advocacy for children. As individuals we are
equipped to offer comfort, give aid and encouragement, and speak on
behalf of and evoke divine help for children.

Individual Christians are constrained by virtue of our faith and
the indwelling of the Holy Spirit to be child advocates. We are also
commissioned corporately, as the church, to advocate on behalf of
children. In the third chapter of the Presbyterian *Book of Order*, the
church is defined as the manifestation in the world of God's intention.

> The Church of Jesus Christ is the provisional demonstration of what
> God intends for all humanity. The Church is called to be a sign in and
> for the world of the new reality . . . (G-3.0200 and G-3.0200a).

Until Christ comes again the church is responsible for bearing witness
to the new reality that is God's intention for the world—a new reality
that does not exclude children. The church has a prophetic role to
play in a world that does not reflect God's intentions, especially in the
lives of children. God did not create children to live in poverty, suffer
abuse and neglect, or be gunned down while playing basketball.
Violence, abuse, and poverty are not the will of God; nor are loneli-
ness, fear, hopelessness, and self-hatred. The church is called to tes-
tify against these things and to a truth that leads to a new reality.

Walter Brueggemann once admonished those preparing for ministry, "Preach the truth as if you are the only one speaking the truth
to the world . . . because, quite frankly, you are."[6] Preaching the
truth can be scary. The prophets in the Bible were not the first ones
on the guest list for dinner parties. Much of this world is already dis-
quieting and on Sunday mornings many of our parishioners, and
sometimes we, would rather not hear more disturbing news, because

when the truth is preached, it can be disturbing. So how are we to gird ourselves for the task of preaching the truth for children—and for its consequences? "Stick to the text. If it is in the Scriptures they [church members] really have no grounds for argument."[6] We would do well, as the church, to remember that we are not called to success or even survival. We are called to faithfulness. Let us be faithful for children.

The Where of Child Advocacy

The church has both an internal and an external life. The internal life of the church is focused on building up the community of faith, nurturing believers, shaping disciples, equipping the saints for ministry, and providing refuge for those who are tired and thirsty. The external life of the church revolves around spreading the gospel, furthering the kingdom, and carrying out Christ's mission in the world. The two cannot and should not be separated. They are two parts of the one reality of a faithful church. The internal and external life of the church helps identify for us the "where" of child advocacy. Child advocacy is carried out internally, within the community of faith, and externally, beyond the church walls in the community of the world.

Advocacy Concerns within the Church

Every action taken, each event planned, every decision made, and each interaction with a child communicates to the children of the church. When the worship service and church school are scheduled at the same time, children learn that worship is for adults only. When fellowship is held in the parlor and refreshments are served on fine china at tables that are adult height, children learn that the church is a place for adults, and they have to fit in to participate. Ministry with children takes place throughout the life of the congregation, and each aspect of that ministry needs to be assessed honestly to make child advocacy a reality within the community. One approach for this assessment is to tap into the structure of the church and have each committee review its work in light of the needs of children. Setting aside a time dedicated to this assessment, in and of itself, will communicate the importance of children. The following questions provide a good place to start in the assessment process.

- In what ways are we welcoming children?
- Are there stumbling blocks for children in our ministry that we need to remove?

- How is the work of this committee helping to shape the faith and identity of young disciples?
- In what ways is the work of this committee advocating for children?
- In what ways can we enhance our child advocacy within the church?

The pastoral care needs of children are as important as the pastoral care needs of adults. In my experience in a multistaff setting, the children too often saw the person who did the primary preaching as their parents' pastor rather than their own. One of our theological grounding points is that we are known by name. In a multistaff setting, every staff person needs to work to learn children's names. Church leaders need to develop relationships with children that are independent of relationships with parents so that children know who they can turn to in times of need.

In recent years churches have been awaking to the importance of protecting children when they are in the church's care. According to the video *Reducing the Risk of Child Sexual Abuse in Your Church*,[7] in the decade preceding 1993, there was a 3000 percent increase in lawsuits filed against churches, and a 5000 percent increase in damages awarded. Reported incidences of abuse of children by clergy have risen dramatically, and the need to protect children and those who work with them is undeniable. In the past decades, many organizations such as Girl and Boy Scouts, Boys and Girls Clubs, and Big Brothers and Sisters have all initiated stronger requirements for screening volunteers and have set guidelines for appropriate interactions. Places where adults have unfettered access to children have been limited. The church remains one of the last places where perpetrators of child abuse have easy entry. Parents who spend hours during the week researching child care centers for their children often freely hand over their children to the church nursery worker or Sunday school teacher. They do so not because they suddenly develop a disregard for their children, but because they trust the church to care enough to look out for their children's interest. This is a sacred trust.

The natural inclination may be to say, "It would never happen in our church." The harsh reality is that one in four girls and one in six boys are abused by the time they reach eighteen, and much of this abuse will occur in religious organizations that rely on the premise that it could not happen there. "It would never happen here" needs to become "We will not let it happen here." While nothing is foolproof, a well-designed child protection policy that is consistently followed goes a long way toward preventing abuse. According to Preferred Risk and Church Mutual insurance companies, the time is coming when churches will not be insurable unless they have a child protection policy. The child is the primary victim when abuse occurs and no monetary amount can compensate for the life-long consequences of abuse. There are secondary victims when a child is abused, and the policy serves to protect them as well. The family who entrusted the child to the church's care is victimized, the church is victimized, and ultimately, the One who came to us as a child and whose name we proclaim is victimized by the violation of little ones. The Child Protection Policy protects the child and the church.

Although child protection policies will vary in length and content, the following components are essential.

- Worker screening: formal application; criminal history background check; reference check; interview; six-month rule; orientation
- Supervision: two-adult rule; windows in doors; parental permission to be alone with youth; adequate staffing during events
- Reporting process: recognizing abuse; where and how to report abuse; protection for good faith reporting

Several good resources are available to help congregations move through the process of developing a child protection policy. Educating the session, the pastors, the congregation, and volunteers about the need for a child protection policy is essential. The video *Reducing the Risk of Child Sexual Abuse in Your Church* takes a business approach to the issue. *Hear Our Cries: Religious Responses to Child Abuse,* a video documentary and study guide on the role of pastors, teachers, counselors, and parents in preventing all forms of abuse, is available from denominational resource centers and the Center for the Prevention of Sexual and Domestic Violence in Seattle, Washington.[8] The booklets *We Won't Let it Happen Here*[9] and *Safe Sanctuaries: Reducing the Risk of Child Abuse in the Church*[10] are also good resources. Middle governing offices may have sample policies on file that churches can use as models.

Advocacy Concerns in the World

Advocating for children outside church walls is essential. The world is in urgent need of the prophetic witness of the church as the voice for millions of voiceless children. Time is a precious commodity in our busy lives. Most of us long for some extra time. What would we do with an extra hour— worship, read a good book, take a walk, write a letter, clean the oven, wash the car? Within that same hour 327 children would be reported abused or neglected, 180 children would be arrested, 77 babies would be born into poverty, and 60 babies would be born without health insurance.[11] The vast majority of us live our lives unaware of the plight of children in our nation. When an event such as the school shootings at Columbine or Paducah occur, we are shocked and for awhile focus attention on children and violence. Yet, *every* day five children or teens commit suicide, nine children or teens are homicide victims, and 180 children are arrested for violent crimes. Every two days, eighteen children—the same number needed to play a baseball game—die in violence. How would we react if every other morning, the news reported the homicides of a baseball field full of players? What will it take for us to be moved to action?

Money is also a precious commodity in our society. The United States is the world leader in military technology and exports, in gross domestic product, in the number of millionaires and billionaires, in health technology, and in defense expenditures, but we spend relatively little on the protection of our children. For example, millions of children run the risk of losing their hearing, their breath, or even their life because they live without adequate health care. Many parents earn too much money to be eligible for Medicaid but not enough to afford medical insurance. Even those who are eligible for Medicaid may have difficulty finding doctors who will accept Medicaid patients. The amount of reimbursement a doctor receives for treating Medicaid patients is lower than with Medicare patients, so there are fewer doctors willing to serve children on Medicaid. Our priorities are askew. Do we have the will to reset our priorities according to God's will?

Whether we choose to act in our neighborhoods, cities, states, nation, or world, we must act. Although the range of problems can seem overwhelming, attention to individual issues can have a broad effect. For example, providing affordable quality child care, equality of education in public schools, violence prevention, or adequate health care each would go a long way to stem the tide of a wide range of problems. An informed process of discernment will help individuals and congregations determine where to focus their action. Organizations such as the Children's Defense Fund are excellent resources for information on issues. Web sites, action alerts, updates, and newsletters from the Washington office of the Children's Defense Fund, as well as CDF's annual publications, are invaluable tools for exploring child advocacy. Informational charts are provided in an appendix at the end of this chapter. Statistics, however, will remain numbers on a page unless presented in language that connects them to peoples lives. Interpreting statistics in the language of faith and the language of people's daily lives will make real the plight of the persons represented by the numbers.

The How of Child Advocacy

Charity or Justice

Church people are familiar with charity. We supply food pantries, volunteer at homeless shelters, and send money from our benevolence budgets. Yet, we are often infected with the piety common in our culture whose mantra is individualism. Our attitude toward recipients of our charity is often pitying and belies a pride that suggests we would never be in such need. We pride ourselves on our ability to make it on our own. This perspective has no place among people of faith because it is a denial of the communal nature of humanity and ultimately a denial of God. None of us truly makes it on his or her own. There is always a host of people who cared for, guided, and nurtured us, who took a chance on us, opened doors for us, or held up a vision of possibility for us. And always, there is God who created, redeemed, and sustains us. Members of the early church were utterly aware of this as the book of Acts, chapter 2, records.

> Awe came upon everyone, because many wonders and signs being done by the apostles. All who believed were together and had all things in common; they would sell their possessions and goods and distribute the proceeds to all, *as any had need* (Vss. 43-45, emphasis mine).

Was this a radical new concept? No. This communal perspective is rooted in the Old Testament. Consider the words attributed to Moses as he describes how the people of God are to live together in their new community.

> If there is among you anyone in need, a member of your community in any of your towns within the land that the LORD your God is giving you, do not be hard-hearted or tight-fisted toward your needy neighbor. You should rather open your hand, willingly lending enough to meet the need, whatever it may be. Be careful that you do not entertain a

mean thought, thinking, "The seventh year, the year of remission is near," and therefore view your needy neighbor with hostility and give nothing; your neighbor might cry to the LORD against you, and you would incur guilt. Give liberally and be ungrudging when you do so, for on this account the LORD your God will bless you in all your work and in all that you undertake. Since there will never cease to be some in need on the earth, I therefore command you, "Open your hand to the poor and needy neighbor in your land" (Deut. 15: 7–11).

The English word "charity" comes from the Latin *caritas*, which means affection. The word charity is not found in contemporary Bible translations. It was used in the King James Version of the Bible to translate the Greek word *agape*, which means self-giving, grace-embodying love. There is no good English word equivalent for *agape*, but love, mercy, and kindness are sometimes used. True charity, mercy, or love means participating in acts and ministries of compassion, such as sponsoring after-school programs, mentoring youth, providing recreational opportunities, supporting immunization clinics, providing scholarships for high-quality child care, tutoring students in inner-city public schools, purchasing coats and school supplies for families in need, filling Thanksgiving baskets, and providing Christmas gifts for children named on angel trees. But acts of kindness are not all that we are called to do.

> He has told you, O mortal, what is good; and what does the LORD require of you but to do justice, and to love kindness and to walk humbly with your God? (Micah 6:8)

God calls us also to do justice. Doing justice means changing the conditions that create the need for angel trees, Thanksgiving baskets, and volunteering in inner-city schools. Justice means making sure inner city school districts have the same funds as suburban school districts. Justice means reducing the gap between the rich and the poor so that everyone is paid a living wage. Justice means assuring that all children have access to affordable, high-quality, early childhood development programs. Doing justice means manifesting Gods life-giving love not only to individuals, but also within the structures of society. "Charity" without justice is incomplete.

The Four-Part Harmony of Child Advocacy

There are many facets to child advocacy. It takes many shapes and forms. We can, for example, understand faith-based child advocacy as a song. An individual can sing the melody or one strand of a song and it can be beautiful. But when it is sung in four-part harmony, the song can become breathtaking when the total becomes more than the sum of the individual parts. The four parts of faith-based child advocacy are direct service, education, systemic change, and spiritual disciplines. When they are used together, the result can be world changing.

Direct Service

A child comes to you with a bleeding cut. The immediate need is to stop the bleeding and bandage the cut. Similarly, direct service activities such as volunteering in shelters, serving in soup kitchens, donating clothes and toys, and providing well-baby clinics help with immediate needs. Jesus invites us, as he did Thomas, to put our hands on the places of pain, and this is what we do in direct service. Direct service, however, affects the least amount of long-term change. These activities can become vital entry points for child advocacy, providing opportunities for hands-on ministries and highlighting areas in need of social change.

Education

The task of educating others allows a child advocate to enhance the workforce for children. The person in the pew may not be aware of the problems facing an enormous number of children. It is the role of the faith-based child advocate to teach members of the congregation about the realities of children's lives, about the mandates of the faith, and about ways to become involved in making a difference for children. This educational activity can take many forms. Adult church school provides a good opportunity for short-term educational programs on child poverty, children and health care, violence prevention, or child care. A series on the implications of baptismal vows for children in crisis that precedes a baptismal service can help authenticate the sacrament and lead to new avenues of ministry. Sponsoring a forum for the broader community on what each major faith tradition teaches about children and justice may provide the starting place for an interfaith community center for teens. Whatever the event, it is important that the three elements of the plight of children, the theological commission, and suggested avenues for faithful response be presented.

Systemic Change

> Woe to the legislators for infamous laws, to those who issue tyrannical decrees, who refuse justice to the unfortunate and cheat the poor among my people of their rights, who make widows their prey and rob the orphan (Isa. 10: 1–2 NJB).

Working for effective change for a large percentage of children requires involvement in the public arena. Addressing the root causes of poverty, racism, and violence are necessary if we are to eradicate these plights. Holding our government to God's higher standards is not a new concept within the Reformed tradition. Both John Calvin and the Westminster Confession issue this call. Wherever a government abandons the common good—and this is inevitable as governments are made up of human beings who are prone to self-centeredness—Christians are duty-and-faith- bound to call our leaders to account and try to make changes in societal structures. When the intersection of faith and citizenship is taken seriously, responsible participation in the public arena becomes imperative. Feeding hungry children is essential. Changing social structures that precipitate hunger means that the child fed today may not be hungry tomorrow and that the child *not* fed today may have hope for tomorrow.

Spiritual Disciplines

Faithful discipleship as manifested in child advocacy is not easy. The only way to have the energy, strength, and wisdom to carry out this essential calling is to be regularly engaged in spiritual disciplines. Participation in prayer, Bible study, mutual accountability, discernment, devotional reading, and other classical spiritual disciplines will undergird activity on behalf of children, as will focusing on children in special times in the church year. The Children's Defense Fund sponsors a national observance of Children's Sabbath every year on the third weekend of October. With its anticipation of the incarnate God who came to us as a child born to a poor family, Advent is an ideal time to focus on children and poverty. Lent provides an opportunity to reflect on and repent from participation in oppressive structures that keep children hungry, hopeless, and voiceless. Focusing through personal devotion and corporate worship on the Author of our compassion for children will keep us humble and steady in advocacy work.

Building a Mighty Movement for Children

Across our nation the winds of change are blowing and people of every faith are joining together in a movement to make a difference for children. The Children's Defense Fund has launched a movement called "Leave No Child Behind." In 1996, the Bishops of the United Methodist Church issued an Initiative on Children and Poverty. The Presbyterian Church (U.S.A.), which as recently as 1990 had a structural design for mission that did not even mention children, celebrated the Year of the Child from July 2000 to June 2001. The church then turned one into ten and embarked on a Decade of the Child. In conjunction with the Decade of the Child, the Presbyterian Child Advocacy Network is launching a new avenue of congregational child advocacy, *Congregations Covenanting for Children*, which invites congregations to commit ministry that has the potential to transform the lives of children, adults, communities, and the church. This undertaking, which is grounded in theology and rooted in spiritual disciplines, calls for faith to be practiced on behalf of children by congregations who subscribe to the following statement.

Because we believe
- All children are created in the image of God.
- The vows we take in baptism bind us together in a covenant community and call us to faithfulness on behalf of the church universal.
- The transforming welcome of the Lord's Table compels us to welcome children in ways that transform lives.
- God requires us to do justice, love mercy, and walk humbly with our God.

Therefore, we covenant to live into these spiritual disciplines, to
- Pray for children.
- Redouble our efforts to involve children in the worship life of the church.
- Strengthen our ministry with children in Christian education, pastoral care, and spiritual formation.
- Discern our mission in addressing the needs of children near and far.
- Be faithful stewards of our resources for ministry and mission with children.
- Share our experiences with others—upholding and building up one another's ministries.

And practicing our faith by
- Intentionally broadening our embrace to include children of the church, the community, the nation, and the world.
- Participating in ministries consistent with the four-part harmony of child advocacy: education, mercy/direct service, justice/systemic change, and spiritual disciplines.

- Assessing our congregation's holistic ministry with and for children.

This is the Presbyterian Church (U.S.A.)'s expression of an ecumenical movement for children, referred to by some as a "sanctuary movement for children."

The When of Child Advocacy

Addie is fourteen years old in body, six years old in development, and wise beyond years in all the ways that matter. Addie has Pervasive Developmental Disorder. She is a delightful child who keeps our family on its toes. Her best friend is Amanda Littlejohn, whom Addie calls Little Amanda John. Last spring Addie and Amanda were in the Special Olympics. Both competed in several events, one of which was a race in which they were competitors with one another. At the starting line, Addie waved at her parents in the stands, smiled, and admired the medals that hung around her neck. At the announcer's command, the runners took off. With her long legs, Addie was soon in the lead enjoying the shouts of encouragement from onlookers. It wasn't long, however, until Addie realized that Amanda was falling behind, and she began looking over her shoulder and yelling for Amanda to catch up. Amanda worked hard but her short legs just would not carry her any quicker. When her encouragement did not get the job done, Addie turned around, went back, and took Amanda by the arm. They finished the race together.

When is the time to advocate for children? After the bills are paid? After the sanctuary is carpeted? After the meetings are done? After the race is won? No. Ask Addie. The time is now.

APPENDIX

STATISTICAL CHARTS ON CHILDREN IN THE UNITED STATES

Choices: Leave No Child Behind— Preventive Investments That Save Money

Every $1 we spend vaccinating children against measles, mumps, and rubella saves $16 in medical costs to treat those illnesses.

Every $1 invested in the supplemental food program for Women, Infants, and Children (WIC) saves $3 in future costs.

If smoking among pregnant women were reduced by one percentage point, 1,000 babies a year could be saved from being born too small, and $21 million a year could be saved in direct medical costs to care for these infants.

Every $1 invested in quality early childhood care and education saves $7 by increasing the likelihood that children will be literate, employed, and enrolled in postsecondary education and less likely to be school dropouts, dependent on welfare, or arrested for criminal activity or delinquency.

Expanding the availability of child-care subsidies increased poor mothers' work participation rates from 29 percent to 44 percent and near-poor mothers' rates from 43 percent to 57 percent, according to a study by the U.S. General Accounting Office.

The lifetime cost of allowing one child to drop out of high school and into a future of crime can total $1.3–$1.5 million.

The average medical treatment for a gun injury costs $16,500 a person, including the full-time medical costs of patient treatment, emergency transportation, and hospital costs in long-term follow-up care.

Reprinted with permission from the Children's Defense Fund

Choices: Pennies a Day Will Give Hope and Help to Millions of Children Left Behind

For 2 cents a day from every American, we could provide all the recommended vaccines for all children from birth until their second birthday.

For 4 cents a day from every American, we could lift more than 30,000 children out of poverty by continuing to expand the earned income tax credit for working families.

For 6 cents a day from every American, we could provide affordable housing for 1 million low-income families, most of whom pay at least half of their income for shelter.

For 9 cents a day from every American, we could provide Head Start to all eligible pre-school-age children who need it and serve one-quarter of infants and toddlers eligible for Early Head Start.

For 14 cents a day from every American, we could fully insure all the 9.2 million children without health coverage.

For 26 cents a day from every American, we could provide child care assistance to all eligible families who need it, while increasing the quality of care.

Reprinted with permission from the Children's Defense Fund

Each Day in America

5 children or teens commit suicide.

9 children or teens are homicide victims.

9 children or teens are killed by firearms.

34 children or teens die from accidents.

77 babies die.

180 children are arrested for violent crimes.

367 children are arrested for drug abuse.

401 babies are born to mothers who received late or no prenatal care.

825 babies are born at low birth weight (less than 5 1bs., 8 oz.).

1,310 babies are born without health insurance.

1,329 babies are born to teen mothers.

2,019 babies are born into poverty.

2,319 babies are born to mothers who are not high school graduates.

2,543 public school students are corporally punished.*

2,861 high school students drop out.*

3,585 babies are born to unmarried mothers.

4,248 children are arrested.

7,883 children are reported abused or neglected.

17,297 public school students are suspended.*

*Based on calculations per school day (180 days of seven hours each)

Reprinted with permission from the Children's Defense Fund

Moments in America for All Children

Every 9 seconds a high school student drops out.*

Every 11 seconds a child is reported abused or neglected.

Every 20 seconds a child is arrested.

Every 24 seconds a child is born to an unmarried mother.

Every 37 seconds a baby is born to a mother who is not a high school graduate.

Every 43 seconds a baby is born into poverty.

Every minute a baby is born to a teen mother.

Every minute baby is born without health insurance.

Every 2 minutes a baby is born a low birth weight.

Every 4 minutes a baby is born to a mother who received late or no prenatal care.

Every 4 minutes a child is arrested for drug abuse.

Every 8 minutes a child is arrested for violent crimes.

Every 19 minutes a baby dies.

Every 42 minutes a child or teen dies in an accident.

Every 3 hours a child or teen is killed by a firearm.

Every 3 hours a child or teen is a homicide victim.

Every 5 hours a child or teen commits suicide.

Every day a person under the age of 25 dies from HIV infection.

*Based on calculations per school day (180 days of seven hours each)

Reprinted with permission from the Children's Defense Fund

20 Key Facts about American Children

3 in 5 preschoolers have their mothers in the labor force.

2 in 5 preschoolers eligible for Head Start do not participate.

2 in 5 never complete a full year of college.

1 in 3 is born to unmarried parents.

1 in 3 will be poor at some point in childhood.

1 in 3 is behind a year or more at school.

1 in 4 lives with only one parent.

1 in 5 is born to a mother who did not graduate from high school.

1 in 5 children under 3 is poor now.

1 in 6 was born to a mother who did not receive prenatal care in the first 3 months of pregnancy.

1 in 8 has no health insurance.

1 in 8 never graduates from high school.

1 in 8 is born to a teenage mother.

1 in 8 lives in a family receiving food stamps.

1 in 12 has a disability.

1 in 13 was born at low birth weight.

1 in 16 lives in extreme poverty.

1 in 24 lives with neither parent.

1 in 60 sees their parents divorce in any year.

1 in 141 will die before their first birthday.

1 in 1,056 will be killed by firearms before age 20.

Reprinted with permission from the Children's Defense Fund

How America Ranks among Industrialized Countries in Investing in and Protecting Children

1st in military technology

1st in military exports

1st in Gross Domestic Product

1st in the number of millionaires and billionaires

1st in health technology

1st in defense expenditures

10th in eighth-grade science scores

12th in the percentage of children living in poverty

16th in living standards among the poorest one-fifth of children

17th in efforts to lift children out of poverty

17th in low birth weight rates

18th in gap between rich and poor children

21st in eighth-grade math scores

23rd in infant mortality

Last in protecting our children against gun violence

According to the Centers for Disease Control and Prevention, U.S. children under age 15 are:

9 times more likely to die in a firearm accident

11 times more likely to commit suicide with a gun

12 times more likely to die from gunfire

16 times more likely to be murdered with a gun than children in 24 other industrialized countries combined.

Of the 154 members of the United Nations, the United States and Somalia (which has no legally constituted government) are the only two nations that have failed to ratify the U.N. Convention on Rights of the Child.

Black infant mortality rates in our nation's capital exceed those in 56 nations, including Bahamas, Barbados, Fiji, and Jamaica.

Reprinted with permission from the Children's Defense Fund

Protect Children Instead of Guns 2001

The latest deadly numbers about children and gun violence in a single year show:

- 3,365 children and teens were killed by gunfire
- 1,990 were murdered by gunfire
- 1,078 committed suicide with a firearm
- 214 died from an accidental shooting
- 1,934 were white
- 1,301 were black
- 605 were Hispanic
- 488 were under age 15
- 153 were under age 10
- 73 were under age 5
- More children and teens died from gunfire than from cancer, pneumonia, influenza, asthma, and HIV/AIDS *combined.*

Did you know?

- Children are twice as likely as adults to be victims of violent crime and more likely to be killed by adults than by other children.
- 61 percent of the more than 87,000 youths killed by gunfire between 1979 and 1999 were white; 36 percent were black.
- Black children and teens are more likely than whites to be victims of firearm homicide, while white children and teens are more likely than their black counterparts to use a firearm to take their own life.
- The firearm death rate for black males between the ages 15 to 19 is four times that of white males of the same age.
- Boys through age 19 are six times more likely than girls to commit suicide with a firearm.

Data released in 2001 show that in a single year 3,365 children and teens were killed by gunfire in the United States—that is one child every two and a half hours, 9 children every day, and more than 60 children every week. And every year, four to five times as many children and youth killed by gunfire suffer from nonfatal firearm injuries.

Despite these alarming numbers, child and youth gun deaths are on the decline. After peaking in 1994 at more than 5,700 young lives, youth firearm deaths have dropped 42 percent overall. Additionally, the number of black children and teens killed by guns has decreased 49 percent, and the number of white children and teens has dropped 36 percent. Although it is encouraging that the number of child gun deaths per year has dropped below 3,500 for the first time since 1987, the number remains disturbingly high. We are still losing too many children. When compared to other industrialized countries, the numbers are even more staggering. According to the Centers for Disease Control and Prevention, the rate of firearm deaths among children under age 15 is almost 12 times higher in the United States than in 25 other industrialized countries combined. American children are 16 times more likely to be murdered with a gun, 11 times more likely to commit suicide with a gun, and nine times more likely to die in a firearm accident than children in these other countries. The needless loss of young lives to gun violence continues to be one of the United States' silent tragedies.

In 1999, homicide accounted for 1,990, or 59 percent of gun deaths among children age 19 and younger. Although most child gun deaths are homicides, two out of every five young firearm deaths are the result of suicide or an accidental shooting. Thirty-two percent of young people killed by guns take their own lives. In 1999, gun suicide accounted for 1,078 child and teen deaths—an average of three young people every day. Guns are used in two out of three youth suicides and, unlike other attempted methods, are the most likely to be fatal. An analysis of state data also shows that children and youth in rural areas are more likely to be victims of gun suicides and accidents, while children and youths in states with large urban populations are more likely to be victims of gun homicides.

Accidental shootings accounted for just over 6 percent of child firearm deaths in 1999; 214 children and teens lost their lives in accidental shootings. As with adolescent suicide, a vast majority of firearms used in unintentional shootings of children and teens come from the victim's home or the home of a relative, friend, or parent of a friend of the victim. A study reported in the *American Journal of Public Health* found that 1.4 million homes with 2.6 million children had firearms that were stored unlocked and loaded or unlocked and unloaded but stored with ammunition. A separate study published in *Injury Prevention* compared firearm ownership in rural and urban areas and found that the prevalence of loaded, unlocked guns in farm households was about twice the level in nonfarm households.

Between 1979 and 1999, gunfire killed more than 87,000 children and teens in America. In the United States, firearms outnumber children by a margin of almost three to one. It is time to stop protecting the approximately 200 million firearms in this country and start protecting the nearly 75 million American children and teens under age 19. It is time to protect children instead of guns.

Reprinted with permission from the Children's Defense Fund

2000 Facts on Child Poverty in America

December 2001

The U.S. Census Bureau considered a three-person family poor in the year 2000 if its annual income was less than $13,738. For a family of four, the poverty threshold was $17,603.

11.6 million American children younger than 18 lived below the poverty line in 2000. Although the number of poor children has fallen for the last seven years due to the strong economy, more children live in poverty today than were poor 20 or 30 years ago.

One out of every six American children (16.1 percent) was poor in 2000. By race and ethnicity, 30.6 percent of black children, 28.0 percent of Hispanic children, 14.4 percent of Asian and Pacific Island children, and 12.9 percent of white children were poor.

The proportion of poor children in working families is at a record high. More than three out of four children in poor families (77 percent) lived with a family member who worked in 2000, up from 61 percent in 1993. One out of three poor children (37 percent) lived with someone who worked full-time year-round. Among poor families with children, the proportion headed by someone who worked is at its highest peak in the 26 years for which these figures are available.

Poor children defy the stereotypes. There are more poor white children (7.3 million) than poor black children (3.5 million) or poor Hispanic children (3.3 million), even though the proportion of black and Hispanic children who are poor is far higher. More poor children live in suburban and rural areas than in central cities. Poor families have 2.3 children on average.

Most child poverty is not temporary. 80 percent of children who are poor one year are also poor the next.

Poverty matters. Poor children are at least twice as likely as nonpoor children to suffer stunted growth or lead poisoning or to be kept back in school. Poor children score significantly lower on reading, math, and vocabulary tests when compared with otherwise-similar nonpoor children. More than half of poor Americans (55 percent) experience serious deprivations during the year (defined as lack of food, utility shutoffs, crowded or substandard housing, or lack of a stove or refrigerator). Poor households are more than 15 times as likely to experience hunger.

Ranked against other social problems, the hazards of poverty are high. A baby born to a poor mother is more likely to die before its first birthday than a baby born to an unwed mother, a high school dropout, or a mother who smoked during pregnancy, according to the Centers for Disease Control. Poverty is a greater risk to children's overall health status than is living in a single-parent family, according to government researchers. Each year spent in poverty adds more to a child's risk of failing to finish high school on time than does living in a single-parent home or being born to a teenage parent, according to data from the U.S. Department of Education.

America can lift more children out of poverty. America cut its child poverty rate in half in the 1960s. Since then, child poverty has grown while national efforts to improve economic security have focused on the elderly. If America lifted low-income children out of poverty in the same proportion as we currently lift low-income seniors, three out of four poor children would no longer be poor.

Reprinted with permission from the Children's Defense Fund

Quality Child Care Helps Parents Work and Children Learn

The need for quality child-care and after-school activities is a daily concern for millions of American parents.

- Every day, 13 million preschoolers including 6 million infants and toddlers are in child care. This amounts to three out of five young children.
- Millions more school-age children and youth are in after-school activities while their parents work. Yet, nearly 7 million children are left home alone after school, during the afternoon hours when juvenile crime peaks and children are vulnerable to risky behavior like smoking, drug and alcohol use, and sexual activity.

Parents need child care to work and support their families.

- Sixty-five percent of mothers with children under age six, and 78 percent of mothers with children ages 6 to 13 are in the labor force.
- In 2000, just one-quarter of all families with children younger than six and only one-third of married-couple families with young children had one parent working and one parent who stayed at home.
- Women bring home half or more of their families' earnings in the majority of U.S. households.
- One out of three children of working mothers are poor even though their mother works or would be poor if their mother did not work.

Good child care is unaffordable for many families, and not enough help is available for them.

- Full-day child care can easily cost between $4,000 and $10,000 a year—at least as much as public college tuition. Yet one-quarter of America's families with young children earn less than $25,000 a year, and a family with both parents working full time at minimum wage earns only $21,400 a year.
- Most low-income families cannot get help paying for child care. Nationally, only one out of seven children eligible under federal law receives help. In two-fifths of the states, a family earning just $25,000 a year would not qualify for assistance.
- One-third of the states place eligible families who apply for help on waiting lists or turn them away without even taking their

names. These families face serious hardships. They struggle to meet their basic needs, often go into debt or may turn to welfare, and are frequently forced to use poor quality child care because they cannot afford better options.

Child care is hard to find.

- Parents in communities across the country have difficulty finding the child care that they need. Families with infants, parents working second or third shift, and parents whose children have special needs face particular challenges finding care.
- A Philadelphia study found that only two out of ten centers were rated as good, with the rest minimally adequate or inadequate. Only 4 percent of family child-care programs were rated as good. Low-income children are often less likely to receive good care.
- A Massachusetts study found that over half of centers serving mostly moderate- to high-income children provided good quality care (57 percent), compared to just one-third of centers serving mostly low-income children (36 percent).
- The number of child-care slots is three times greater in affluent zip codes than in low-income neighborhoods in California, according to a new study. Slots are also limited in moderate-income areas, where families earn too much to qualify for child-care assistance but not enough to afford high-priced care on their own. Overall, the supply of child care has barely kept pace with the growth in the child population.

Child care helps shape children's futures, yet the quality of care for many children is inadequate.

- Research on early brain development and early childhood demonstrates that the experiences children have and the attachments children form early in life have a decisive, long-lasting impact on their later development and learning. High-quality care beginning in early childhood improves children's school success.
- Many children are not getting the good quality care and education they need in their early years to start school ready to learn. Forty-six percent of kindergarten teachers report that half of their class or more have specific problems when entering kindergarten, including difficulty following directions, lack of academic skills, problems in their situations at home, and/or difficulty working independently.

- Good quality child care is hard to find in a marketplace where child-care workers earn an average of just $16,350 a year and typically receive no benefits or paid leave.
- Cosmetologists must attend as much as 2,000 hours of training before they can get a license, yet 30 states do not require teachers in child-care centers to have any early childhood training before they begin working with children.

NOTES

1. Joseph Allen, *Love and Conflict: a Covenantal Model of Christian Ethics* (Nashville: Abingdon, 1984), 20–23.

2. Joseph Allen, *Love and Conflict: a Covenantal Model of Christian Ethics* (Nashville: Abingdon, 1984), 32–38.

3. Joseph Allen, *Love and Conflict: a Covenantal Model of Christian Ethics* (Nashville: Abingdon, 1984, 39–42.

4. *The State of Children in America's Union*, "Choices: Leave No Child Behind—Preventive Investments That Save Money" (Washington, DC: The Children's Defense Fund, 2002) xii.

5. Albert Camus, *Resistance, Rebellion, and Death* (New York: Alfred A. Knopf, 1962) 73.

6. Conversation with Walter Brueggeman, Naples, Florida, 1998.

7. Richard Hammar, *Church Law and Tax Report*, 1993 (Matthews, NC), available by calling (800) 222-1840.

8. The Center for the Prevention of Sexual and Domestic Violence, Seattle, 1992. Phone (206) 634-1903; Web site *www.cpsdv.org*

9. The Child Advocacy Office of the Presbyterian Church (U.S.A.), (888) 728-7228, ext. 5838.

10. Joy Melton (Nashville: Discipleship Resources, 1998), (800) 685-4370; Web site *www.discipleshipresources. org*.

11. *The State of Children in America's Union*, "Moments in America for All Children" (Washington DC: The Children's Defense Fund, 2002), 14.

CHAPTER FIVE

Selecting and Sharing Bibles with Children

Patricia Griggs

The fast-paced, multimedia approach to life that is prevalent today creates a challenge for parents and teachers who want to unlock the treasures of the Bible for children in a way that captures their imaginations. Consider the following characteristics of our age:

- Children are bombarded with the color, sound, and fast pace of television.
- Teachers in public schools have adopted approaches to teaching to meet the needs of the current generation, creating classrooms that are filled with activities, games, and videos.
- Many classrooms have one or more computers, and schools are making computer labs increasingly available to classes as early as kindergarten.
- Many children's days are so scheduled that they are at a loss when left on their own.
- The Bible competes with hundreds of other books.
- For many adults and children, the pace of life has overwhelmed the ability to wonder, contemplate, and know inner peace.

In the face of these realities, church school teachers and parents must do all they can to cultivate children's natural wonder and nourish children's ability to treasure the times when they can "be still and know that I am God" (Ps. 46:10). Yet, they do so in the context of expectations of high-tech, fast-paced education—expectations that are difficult for most church classrooms to meet. Church school teachers face the daunting task of coming up with meaningful, active teaching strategies that make experiences at church special while addressing key questions such as, What makes a story from the Bible more believable and meaningful than a familiar television series about an heroic character? How can I inspire interest in and a sense of reverence for a book that is about people who lived thousands of years ago in a different culture and place? How do I introduce a book—written by and for adults—to children in an age-appropriate, exciting, *and* authentic way? What activities will address not only the multiple intelligences of the children present in the classroom, but also their emotions, hopes, needs, and daily realities?

Opening the Bible with children can feel like an overwhelming or impossible task. The concerns and issues are real; however, they must not be allowed to eclipse the sense of privilege and potential joy inherent in this endeavor. The questions raised above would require a great deal of expertise and experience to answer. In this chapter, we will explore a variety of topics including the role of teachers, giving Bibles to children, and teaching Bible skills. The goal is to stimulate thinking and present some ideas on which to build. The privilege and joy of accompanying children on their journeys of discovery of God's love as it is expressed in Scripture are among the most rewarding experiences for parents and teachers. May God bless every teacher and parent as they open the Bible with children.

Opening the Bible with Children

When teachers and parents open the Bible *with* children, they become both co-learners and editors. The word *with* in the title of this section is intentional. It reflects the presupposition that the child and the adult are learning together—discovering more about God, faith, and all that Scripture holds. Although it is generally true that adults know more about the Bible than do children, it is also true that adults are learners along with children. The journey of faith is not conducted alone but is experienced in community, and children are an essential, valuable part of that community. Wherever there is interaction, learning takes place for both adult and child. This is especially true in matters of faith, which go well beyond the realm of cognition.

Opening the Bible *with* children is characterized by the removal of barriers to understanding, which in turn enables children to enter biblical stories and embark on a journey of discovery. This approach requires that teachers accept the doubts of children, embrace questioning, engage students as values are formed and foundations of faith are established, acknowledge that beliefs mature as children develop, be honest about the limits of their knowledge, and explore various possibilities.

While adults are eager to share the Bible with children, we must not forget that the Bible is a book written about, by, and for adults, so whenever the Bible is opened with children, teachers become editors by being selective about stories, using age-appropriate vocabulary, and determining the emphasis of a given text. Care must be taken not to change the meaning of texts but to present materials in a manner consistent with Scripture and in line with the child's ability to comprehend. In some cases, a teacher may choose to slow down the pace of a given curriculum so that the content matches the developmental stage, ability, and interests of the children. Slowing down allows time for questioning, repetition, and a variety of teaching strategies that enable children to remember and apply the Scriptures to their lives. The emphasis is on the quality of the learning experience rather than the quantity of material. Some general guidelines are presented for opening the Bible with children at different age/grade levels:

Infancy and toddlerhood. Young children may very well have an awareness of God long before they can understand what a Bible is. If a child grows up in a family that is involved in a congregation, he or she will learn through the experiences of celebrations and traditions of the family and the church before being formally introduced to the Bible. If the Bible has a central place in the home and the church, children will naturally come to see it as an integral book for the life of the Christian and will come to associate the Bible with the word of God. The role that Scripture customarily plays in home and church life, as well as its importance during special times such as Advent, Palm Sunday, Easter, and the Lord's Supper, will communicate its importance to the Christian faith.

Preschool. Children's Bible storybooks may be introduced to preschool children, not so they can read them but so that they can look at the large, colorful pictures while the teacher reads or tells the stories. Illustrations will influence a child's conception of God and Jesus and what a child remembers about a given story. Bible storybooks should be chosen with great care. (Guidelines for making selections are discussed below.) A teacher will tell a biblical story while holding an open Bible on his or her lap. Key words such as God, Jesus, love, and faith will begin to be associated with the Bible, as will the teacher's attitude—toward the Bible and toward children. In the early years, children will likely develop a sense of mystery and awe toward the Bible.

Kindergarten and First Grade. As children move into kindergarten and first grade, the teacher introduces a Bible story by explicitly stating that the story is from the Bible and by using the terms New Testament and Old Testament. While the children will not fully understand the concepts New Testament and Old Testament, they will become aware that there are two parts to the Bible. The way the stories are presented can help children begin to make connections between the stories of the Bible and the way people of faith are to live.

Second Grade. Beginning readers are excited about reading and are often eager to read aloud. Even though children are beginning to read well in second grade, being able to read and being able to understand are two different things. Reading does not equal comprehension! It is good to allow children to read aloud, but allowing a beginning reader to introduce a story to a class may cause the children who are listening to become impatient. Poor reading can make a story dull and cause students to lose interest or miss the point. The reader can become discouraged or embarrassed if the words are too difficult. Reading aloud by children can be done after the teacher has presented the story and defined difficult words. It is helpful to choose short verses to be read aloud. Some children are stronger readers than others, so it is important not to neglect weaker readers. Unison reading and pronunciation practice will help equalize reading performance.

Third Grade. Third-graders are capable of reading and understanding many of the stories in the Bible and are enthusiastic about using the Bible. Third-graders are ready to begin developing simple, basic Bible skills, such as looking up verses. Because children at this level love adventure and excitement, this is a good time to introduce some Old Testament stories.

Fourth Grade. At this grade level, children are reading well and are able to apply Scriptures to their own lives. It is appropriate to introduce fourth-graders to simple concordances and age-appropriate Bible dictionaries. In many churches, fourth-graders stay in church for the entire worship service. Consequently, choosing Bible stories that help children understand the drama and purpose of worship is important.

Fifth and Sixth Grades. Fifth- and sixth-graders are ready to master more complicated Bible skills, learn about the origin of the

Bible, begin using Bible resources, and use their developing ability to think abstractly.

Selecting Bibles and Bible Storybooks

When asked what causes them to pick up a Bible storybook and begin to browse through it, many people mention the cover art, title, or author. When asked what they look for when browsing through the book, many will mention illustrations, translation, theology, attractiveness, or publisher. These criteria are good places to start. However, there is more to consider when choosing a Bible or a Bible storybook for children. Always look at the book through the eyes of the child and consider the developmental stages, reading level, and stages of the child's faith development. Ask the following key questions:

1. For whom is the book intended? Consider the age, abilities, and experience of the child. Some children's Bibles will indicate on the cover the age group for which the book is intended. Do not assume this information is applicable to your children. The reading and comprehension level of children—especially younger children—differs even among communities. The age group for which the book is intended may refer to the reading level but not to the concepts, illustrations, size of type, or layout. Take the time to explore all aspects of the book.

2. How will the book be used? Is the book to be read to the children, or are the children expected to read it themselves? Is the book to be used in the classroom? If so, how?

3. Is the book a Bible or is it a collection of Bible stories? If it is a Bible, what translation or paraphrase is it? Choose a Bible translation that is in keeping with your church's tradition. If it is a Bible storybook, are the stories those that you want to present? Are they appropriate for children? Just because a story can be recast in language for children does not mean it is appropriate.

4. Is the content consistent with the Bible the adults use in the congregation? The theology presented in the story should be consistent with that taught in the church. Parents need to feel comfortable with the book, and children should not be faced with conflicts in theology before they are ready to deal with them.

5. Is the paraphrase or retelling imaginative and appealing for children without straying from the essence of the biblical text?

If additions or omissions change the essence of the stories from how they appear in Scripture, the storybook is probably not appropriate.

6. Are the illustrations appropriate? Bright, cartoon-like illustrations may be appealing, but if other books containing such art are known by the child to be fantasy and just for fun, what will make Bible stories seem different? On the other hand, dull, severe illustrations may be frightening or communicate that reading the Bible is a joyless task. Illustrations need to be friendly and accurately communicate what it was like in Bible times along with the events, the emotions, and the essence of the stories in a way that is accessible to children.

7. Is the layout appealing and easy to follow? In some cases, the illustrations and perhaps the content might be appropriate for a given age group, but the layout and size or style of print may not be. Regardless of the age of the reader, if the layout of the book is not user-friendly, it will probably not be read. Consider the size of the print, the font style, the number of words in a sentence, and how the text is organized. For Bibles, ease of locating the separate books of the Bibles is crucial. Contents lists with page numbers, tabs, or color coding can be very helpful. (The ability to find a Bible reference without helps is not a moral triumph; rather, it is simply a skill that some are better at than others.)

8. Are the binding and the paper heavy enough to withstand a lot of use? White Bibles with delicate paper may be attractive, but they may not be the most practical selection for children. All aspects of giving Bibles to children need to communicate the expectation that the Bible will be used—opened and closed, read, studied, and carried to church and Sunday school.

9. Is the vocabulary appropriate for the age of the child? Remember that reading is not the same as comprehension. How many words will need to be explained? How will the concepts be understood? If the book is being used in a classroom setting, understanding hard words and concepts becomes part of the teaching process. If the book is to be read to the child by an adult, the child can ask questions but if the child is reading on his or her own, words and concepts must be clear enough to be understood without explanation. The readability of a book can be determined in several ways:

- Consult a reading specialist or public school teacher.
- Use a readability graph or chart, which a reading specialist would share one with you. Generally speaking, the charts indicate that the fewer words per sentence and fewer syllables per word, the lower the reading level.
- Show the book to several children in the same grade and ask them to read it aloud to you. Then ask questions to see if they comprehended what they read.

With experience, most teachers will learn to determine the readability of a book just by looking at it. Until that experience is gained, it is good to rely on a specialist or specialized tool, especially if multiple copies of a book are being purchased.

Giving Children Bibles from the Church Family

Many churches have a tradition of presenting Bibles to children at particular points in their lives. Decisions that are involved in making this experience a positive one for the child and the church will be discussed below, but first consider the following description offered by a church member of such an event.

> It was obvious that this was going to be a special day at church. There were several stacks of new Bibles on the Communion table, and the excitement of the children was electric. During the service the pastor, the fourth-grade teachers, the elder related to the children's department, and the fourth-grade class came forward. The children stood around the table and looked intently at the Bibles. The pastor spoke to them about when she, like them, stood in front of the church to receive her Bible. She had it with her to show the children. She spoke about how much that Bible has meant to her, and she expressed her hope that the Bible they were to receive that day would have a significant influence on their lives. After the pastor addressed the children, the elder and the teachers joined the pastor in presenting a new Bible to each child. Every child opened the Bible immediately upon returning to the group, looking at the inscription that had been written on the inside cover. Many of the children stood hugging their Bibles to their chests as a prayer was offered after all the Bibles had been given out.
>
> When the children returned to their seats, the first thing each did was show the Bible to the person sitting next to him or her. Most of the children received a hug and a big smile in return. When it was time for the Scripture reading, the pastor encouraged people to find the passage using the pew Bibles or, in the children's case, to use their new Bibles. The page numbers where the passages could be

found were included in the bulletin, and sufficient time was allowed for everyone to find the passage before the pastor began to read.

Notice some key things that happened in this service:

- The Bibles were prepared and displayed on a table.
- The teacher, the pastor, and someone from the children's committee were all involved, communicating that the gift was from the whole congregation.
- The pastor recalled receiving her Bible and shared what it meant to her.
- A personalized inscription was included in each Bible.
- The event was important enough to be included in the worship service, and prayer was offered for the children.
- The pastor provided the opportunity during the reading of Scripture for the children to use their Bibles, giving them time to find the passage and follow along.
- The page number for the Scripture passage was printed in the bulletin.
- The service was special for the children who received Bibles and for the whole congregation.

When planning to present Bibles to children, it is wise to have a small group of people responsible for selecting the Bibles, to inform the children's families, and to prepare the children and teachers for the event. In preparation for the event, the following questions need to be addressed:

1. Why are we giving Bibles to children?
   Some possible answers are: it is a tradition; it is a good way for the church to show the children that the congregation cares about them; parents expect it; the children have siblings who have received Bibles in the past and would be hurt if they did not receive one; children like to bring their own Bibles to church; teachers can ask the children to read a story, have devotions, or prepare ahead of time at home if they know the children have their own Bibles; and having a Bible is important to the spiritual development of children. Knowing why you are giving out Bibles will help guide the entire process. The reasons for giving Bibles will also help determine the appropriate age group to receive them and may even indicate that there is more than one time in children's lives when the church may want to give Bibles.

2. At what age/class will we give Bibles?

Infant baptism; third, fourth, or fifth grades; youth confirmation; and high school graduation all provide good opportunities to give Bibles.

Infant baptism. An illustrated Bible storybook can be given to a family of a child at the time of baptism with encouragement to read the stories to the child. A good time for the presentation is just before the elder hands the baptismal certificate to the parents. The book may be presented to the family by a fourth- or fifth-grade volunteer representing the children of the congregation. A teacher can help by attaching to the cover a sticky note with a sentence or two that the presenter can read before handing the Bible storybook to the family. (e.g., "On behalf of the children of [church name], I wish to present this Bible storybook to [child's name]." Allow the presenter to practice a few times before the service begins.

Third, fourth, or fifth grade. Giving Bibles at this stage honors children's developing reading abilities. Providing Bibles at the age when children are first expected to participate in the full worship hour is a good way to celebrate this transition as a happy milestone. The goal is to provide children with a Bible that is easily read and will cultivate their Bible skills, such as looking up verses and using study helps. A Bible that includes word lists, cross-references, short introductory articles and outlines for each book, footnotes, and maps is a good choice for this age group.

Confirmation or high school graduation. Teenagers will need a good study Bible that will last until adulthood. The gift of a Bible is a good way to mark these passages into adulthood. A Bible that has footnotes, cross-references, maps, a concise concordance, a glossary, study notes, and essays is a good choice for recognizing the ability of youth to study the Bible in depth.

3. When will the Bibles be given out?

Bibles will be used in teaching regardless of whether they are the property of the church or of the students, and teachers will introduce Bible skills regardless of when Bibles are received. When Bibles are given is important in relation to the total experience of the children, so it is important to consider the background, schedules, home life, and educational and church experiences of *your* children when making this decision. Here are some considerations:

The Beginning of the School Year

- Enthusiasm is high.
- Students will be able to use their own Bibles all year.
- Children's reading and other skills will not be as strong as they will in the spring.
- The curriculum will need to be adjusted so that the children will be able to use their Bibles all year.

The End of the School Year

- Second- and third-graders will have improved reading skills.
- Time will need to be allowed for teachers to respond to the initial enthusiasm the children have when they receive their Bibles and to introduce some new Bible skills
- Giving Bibles can serve as a climax to the year of preparation for confirmation.

Special Seasons in the Church Year

- Children will associate receiving their Bibles with that celebration every year.
- Advent is a good time for reading familiar stories.
- Lent is a good time to encourage daily individual or family devotional reading.
- Palm Sunday and Pentecost are celebrations that can be enriched by the presentation of Bibles.

4. Which version of which translation of the Bible will be given? Several factors affect the selection of a Bible version, including the reading and comprehension level of the recipients, the traditions of the church, and the purpose for giving the Bible. There are many different English translations and versions of the Bible because the original texts were written in Hebrew, Aramaic, and Greek, and in keeping with the call of the Protestant Reformation to make Scripture available in the language of the people. Advances in scholarship, as well as changes in contemporary language and culture, provide impetus for the production of new versions of the Bible. Finally, in some cases, a particular Bible serves to support a particular ideological perspective.

Reading the introduction to a Bible version will provide insight into the process, purpose, intention, and credentials of the translation committee and thereby aid in selection. In some cases, the primary goal is to produce a Bible that renders as closely as possible a word-for-word translation from the original languages. Since these translations are more literal, they can be more difficult for young readers than Bible translations and paraphrases that reflect contemporary idioms. The American Standard Version is an example of this type of Bible. The New Revised Standard and the Contemporary English versions reflect a concern for accurate translation, while at the same time using contemporary style and language. Paraphrases, such as *The Living Bible*, provide a contemporary rendition of Scripture that reflects the interpretation of scholars who "unpack" words and concepts in an effort to make them more accessible to readers. Some Bibles have words believed to be spoken by Jesus in red ink; however, it is important to keep in mind that the text is not always clear and scholars are not in agreement about which words Jesus spoke.

The persons responsible for choosing the Bible that will be given need to make an informed choice. A visit to a bookstore to review a wide variety of Bibles is in order. A photocopiable checklist for comparing Bibles is provided on page 125 of this resource. Many religious bookstores also have a Bible comparison chart that can be helpful.

5. How will teachers and parents prepare for this event?
   Generally, children are very excited about receiving their own Bibles and want to begin reading right away. Because most books are read from beginning to end, children often want to start at Genesis 1:1, intending to read straight through. This can pose some problems. Not all of the stories in Genesis are appropriate for children. They contain adult concepts, difficult language, and unfamiliar names that can discourage or even frighten young readers. In one church, a parent called the church a few weeks after her third-grade son had received his Bible. The boy had been faithful in his reading and had made his way through a good part of the beginning of Genesis. The trouble was that he was having nightmares because the stories he had read portrayed a vengeful God and sinful, violent people. The parent was faced with a very difficult situation because neither her son nor she had received any direction for selecting stories to read.

The Bible is not like other books. It is a collection of books with diverse types of literature that do not follow in chronological order. Teachers and parents need to prepare ahead of time to provide guidance to recipients of new Bibles, but too often the giving of Bibles is treated as something the church does that is separate from what happens in church school or at home. Teachers are often focused on a curriculum that does not allow time to deal with the reception of Bibles for more than one Sunday, and parents, who often feel inadequate to guide their children in Bible reading, may assume that since the children are going to church school, they are receiving adequate guidance. There are many ways teachers and parents can be helped to support each other and nurture children during this time. Most important is contact between a church representative (director of Christian education, Sunday school superintendent, chair of the Christian education committee, pastor, and/or church school teacher) and parent(s) or guardian(s). A parent's meeting is ideal, but if this is not possible, home visits, phone calls, or letters can accomplish many of the goals, which may include:

- confirming the spelling of the child's name
- providing parent(s) or guardian(s) with the date for giving out Bibles and other pertinent information
- explaining why Bibles are being given to this particular group
- providing a rationale for the Bible version that has been chosen
- reviewing developmental issues and realistic expectations for the children receiving Bibles
- providing a list of Scripture readings appropriate for the age group
- providing a list of Scripture passages on which future lessons will be based
- providing suggestions for ways to encourage Bible reading at home, such as setting aside daily time to read with children or inviting (not requiring) the child to read a passage as part of table grace at dinnertime
- experiencing sample activities that the children will engage in at church school as they become acquainted with their new Bibles
- creating a list, with parents' input, of other Bible-reading activities that can be done at home

- addressing parents' or guardians' questions and concerns
- stressing the importance of parents' or guardians' attitudes in forming a child's attitude toward the Bible
- creating a shared sense of excitement among parents/ guardians, teachers, and all those involved in this event

6. What will be done to prepare and support the children in Bible ownership? If a Bible is not read, learned, and lived, the act of giving and receiving Bibles is reduced to one that is symbolic or even magical. Here are some suggestions for preparing children for and supporting them in Bible ownership:

Prepare the classroom. Take an inventory of the Bibles and Bible study resources in the classroom, removing unused books and adding what is necessary. Many churches have older Bibles that have been on classroom shelves for years. Neglected Bibles speak loudly to children of the importance—or lack of importance—of the Bible to churches. It is essential to have on hand copies of the same version of the Bible that children will be given for visitors or for those who do not bring their Bibles. Children will be encouraged to bring the Bibles they receive to church school; however, some children will have more support at home than others will, so no one should be shamed for not bringing a Bible. This will be a good time to inventory all of the classrooms and see that each has what it needs. It is easier to teach basic Bible skills when all the students are using the same version and edition because the books will have the same layout, making it easier to direct the children. Teens will benefit from having a variety of translations on hand to use in Bible study. Beginning with the fifth- and sixth-grade classrooms, study helps such as atlases, concordances, and dictionaries should be available.

Tell the children. As obvious as this sounds, children are often the last to know when an event is being planned for them. If the same grade has been receiving Bibles for years, many children will know when they are going to receive Bibles. Nonetheless, it is important to treat the children with the same respect their parents or guardians are given, providing them with the details of the event and emphasizing that this is a momentous occasion, not just for them but for the whole church.

Plan a Bible day at church. Encourage members to bring Bibles that are special to them to display. Be sure to label the Bibles before placing them on tables in the narthex or in the fellowship hall so that persons looking at them know to whom the

Bibles belong. The church service that day can focus on some aspect of the formation of the Bible or on the sharing of the Bible through missions. People could also be given the opportunity to share the importance of their Bibles to them. The purpose is to highlight the importance of personal Bibles to the adults in the congregation and develop a sense of anticipation for the children.

Plan a special time with the pastor. Many pastors will welcome the opportunity to meet with children on the children's own turf. If church school meets at the same time as worship and there is only one pastor, it may take some creativity to figure out how the pastor can meet with the children, but the pastor's presence will enhance the sense of importance of the coming event in children's lives. The pastor can provide the details of what will happen in the church service. The children will be more relaxed about the service if they know what to expect and if they have had a comfortable and fun encounter with the pastor. The pastor might also share some of his or her experiences with the Bible or bring a variety of Bibles for the children to explore, then explain why a particular version was chosen for them. Greek and Hebrew editions, with a sample reading and learning a few Hebrew or Greek words, may spark children's interest in Bible study.

Prepare reading lists. A reading list should have the title of the selection if there is one, the Bible reference, and a short statement telling what the story or passage is about. A couple of questions to be discussed in church school may also be included. Narratives work best to capture children's imaginations, but there are also other considerations, such as:

- What Scripture passages will be read during worship?
- What stories are going to be included in the curriculum in the next few months?
- Are there stories that are particularly appropriate for children that are not being included in the curriculum or in the worship services?
- Are there short passages that would be appropriate for memorization?
- Are there appropriate narratives for the children to read that will enhance the celebration and understanding of the seasons of the church year?

- What books of the Bible does the church community consider priority for the children to become familiar with?

Plan Bible-related lessons. A few sessions should be dedicated to helping the children become acquainted with how the Bible is organized and how to look up verses. They should not be embarrassed to use the table of contents. Use basic Bible skills throughout the year in order that children learn them so well the skills become automatic and those who enter the class during the year can be brought up to speed.

Coordinate worship opportunities with activities in the classroom. Coordinating worship and classroom activities will reinforce Bible skills. When church school precedes worship, the teacher can introduce the Scripture passage and help the children find it in their Bibles. If church school follows worship, the Scripture can be reviewed and time can be allowed for addressing questions that arose. When Scripture is read in the worship service, it is important that the reference be listed in the bulletin and both it and the page number be announced. Providing both visual and auditory signals will reinforce Bible skills, and the easier it is to find a passage, the more likely children will be to use their Bibles during worship. Here are some other suggestions for coordinating Bible use in worship with church school:

- Occasionally provide the opportunity for a child to participate in worship leadership by reading Scripture during the worship service. Be sure to give the passage to the child ahead of time and make sure the reading is well practiced, not only at home, but also using the microphone in front of people in the sanctuary.
- Have the class prepare a choral reading of a Scripture passage or a pantomime to present in the service.
- Have the class make a banner based on a Scripture passage to be displayed in the sanctuary during worship.
- After studying a passage, invite the children to create illustrations to be used as bulletin covers, or include several illustrations along with the children's interpretive remarks as a bulletin insert.
- Distribute activity sheets that may include questions to be answered as the child listens to the sermon, a crossword

puzzle or word game, and vocabulary lists for the children to work on during the service. Some churches provide "worship kits" for children that contain an activity sheet, pencil, note pad, crayons, numbered bookmarks, and a special children's bulletin that has the numbers 1, 2, 3, 4, and so on written next to hymns and readings to correspond to the bookmarks.

Integrating Bible Skills with Curriculum Materials

For students to learn there must be repetition, relevance, a variety of activities (see chapter 3, page 51 on multiple intelligences), and success. At the beginning of the church school year, teachers need to determine which skills will be taught, when they will be taught, how they will be taught, and how each skill can be practiced within the context of the church school curriculum materials. It is helpful if the Christian education committee, along with the director of Christian education, the church school superintendent, and church school teachers work together to develop a Bible skills education schedule with specific objectives to guide the Bible education endeavor. A sample schedule is provided at the end of this discussion, along with a skills chart; however, there may be other skills that your faith community wants the children to learn. Moreover, there is a great variance in ability from one school district to another, from one group of children to another, and from one child to another. The skill schedule needs to be flexible and reflect the developing skills of the children, the demands of the church school curriculum materials, and the abilities of the church school teachers. When choosing which Bible skills to teach, it is important to be selective and not try to teach all Bible skills in one year.

In order to know which Bible skills are appropriate for a particular class, the teacher needs to know what reference skills are being taught and used in public school at each grade level. For children to understand the difference between Old and New Testaments, they need to have a sense of time and history—a skill usually acquired in third or fourth grade; for children to appreciate Bible maps, they need the global concepts of space and direction as well as an understanding of boundaries and the political concepts of cities, states, countries, and empires—skills generally developed in fifth grade; and using footnotes requires the advanced reading skills developed in grades seven and above.

Input from a school teacher will be invaluable for developing a Bible skills schedule. If during the course of the church school year children need a great deal of help, ask many questions, and seem to struggle with the tasks assigned to them, the skills required for the tasks are probably new to them and the schedule will need to be revised. Nothing deters learning more than unrealistic expectations. Determining the ability of the students takes some time. Since there are a variety of abilities within any given group, smaller classes will be more effective than larger ones.

The Bible skills education schedule needs to correlate with the church school curriculum materials so that skills are practiced within the context of each lesson. Curriculum materials that place more emphasis on the content and structure of the Bible will facilitate the teaching of Bible skills to a greater extent than materials that feature contemporary issues and interpersonal relationships, but there are ways to incorporate Bible skills into most lessons. Here are some suggestions:

- If the lesson refers to more than one recounting of a given event, such as the resurrection, encourage the use of cross-reference notes and concordances to find the other passages.
- Concordances and Bible dictionaries can be used to seek out other passages related to the theme of a given lesson.
- Bible dictionaries can be used to look up the key words.
- When customs, traditions, locations, or groups of people are mentioned, more information can be sought in Bible dictionaries and encyclopedias, Bible introductions, and Old and New Testament histories.

It is important also to be realistic about expectations placed on church school teachers. Many church school teachers are not professionally trained as teachers, and for those who are, introducing dictionary use, alphabetizing, categorizing, or sequencing skills to children is not what they need to be about in church school. It is best for religious education to build on the basic skills that children are learning in school. Church school teachers will need to find creative ways to introduce and reinforce each Bible skill. Games, charts, projects, crossword puzzles, worksheets, jigsaw puzzles, manipulatives, scavenger hunts, and computer programs all make learning fun. Some curriculum materials provide activities. When they are not provided, teachers will need to be creative and develop activities.

Sometimes a small group of adults is willing to take on this task as their way of supporting the church school.

Sample Objectives for Grade Levels

First Grade:
- By midyear, children will read simple verses.
- By the end of the year, children will know there are two main parts: one (the Old Testament, or Hebrew Scriptures) is about people and events before Jesus was born; and one is about Jesus, his followers, and the early church (the New Testament).
- By the end of the year, children will know the names of the four Gospels and be able to state that the word "gospel" means good news.

Second Grade:
- Children will read simple passages aloud as well as sections in Bible storybooks.
- Children will recognize that the Bible is about God, Jesus, and the relationships God has with people and the rest of creation.
- Children will begin to be able to identify stories as being from the Old Testament or New Testament.
- Children will be introduced to the fact that the Bible contains different types of literature, such as history, stories, letters, laws, and psalms, which are poems that were often sung as part of worship.

Third Grade:
- Children will be able to look up verses.
- Children will recognize some of the common abbreviations for books of the Bible.
- Near the end of the year, children will be introduced to cross-reference notes.

Fourth Grade:
- Children will be introduced to concordances and Bible dictionaries.
- Children will know how to use cross-reference notes.

Fifth Grade:
- Children will use Bible atlases.
- Children will identify Bible books by type.

Sixth Grade:
- Children will develop mastery with concordances, dictionaries, and atlases.

• Children will be introduced to the history of the Bible and its development.

A Checklist for Comparing Bibles

Bible version:

1. Did an individual or a committee do the translation? (A committee usually shows less theological bias, especially if it crosses denominational lines.)
2. Is the translation an authorized one? If so, by whom?
3. What is indicated as the purpose of the translation in the introduction or preface?
4. Are the format, paper, and binding appropriate for the age group and intended usage?
5. Are the layout and typeface easy to read?
6. How easy is it to find chapter and verse numbers?
7. Is poetry set differently from prose?
8. What study helps are included?

    footnotes _____

    cross-reference cites _____

    concordance _____

    word list/glossary _____

    illustrations _____

    maps _____

    introductions to books _____

    articles _____

    outlines of books _____

    other _____

9. What style of language is used?

    poetic _____

    contemporary _____

    inclusive language when referring to human beings _____

10. Is it a revision of a translation or a new translation?
11. Is the cover attractive and durable?

SELECTED RESOURCES

This list is not meant to be comprehensive, but to suggest books that might be helpful to those selecting Bibles, Bible storybooks, and Bible resource books.

Bibles and Bible Storybooks

Augsburg Story Bible, Chicago: Augsburg Press, 1992

Living God's Way, Kelowna, BC: Wood Lake Books, 1994

Holy Bible: Children's Illustrated Edition, Nashville: Thomas Nelson Publishers, 1998

Toddlers' Action Bible, St. Louis, MO: Concordia Publishing House, 1998

The Children's Bible in 365 Stories, Oxford, UK: Lion Publishing, 2001

The Doubleday Illustrated Children's Bible, New York: Doubleday, 1983

The Family Story Bible, Louisville, KY: Westminster John Knox Press, 1996

The Young Reader's Bible, Cincinnati, OH: Standard Publishing, 1998

Reference Books

Bible Dictionary: A First Reference Book, Cincinnati, OH: Standard Publishing, 1995

Bible Encyclopedia: A First Reference Book, Cincinnati, OH: Standard Publishing, 1995

Children's Atlas of the Bible, Hauppauge, NY: Barron's Juveniles, 1997

Children's Bible Dictionary, Hauppauge, NY: Barron's Juveniles, 1998

Children's Guide to the Bible, Grand Rapids: Zondervan Publishing House, 1998

International Children's Bible Dictionary, Nashville: Word Publishing, 1997

International Children's Bible Handbook, Nashville: Word Publishing, 1997

Kidcordance: Big Ideas from the Bible and Where to Find Them, Grand Rapids: Zondervan Publishing House, 1999

Let's Explore Inside the Bible, Chicago: Augsburg Press, 1994

The Baker Bible Dictionary for Kids, Grand Rapids: Baker Book House, 1997

What the Bible Is About, for Young Explorers, Ventura, CA: Gospel Light, 1986

CHAPTER SIX

Child Care and Weekday Education in Churches

Mary Anne Fowlkes

Why Would Churches Provide Child Care and/or Weekday Programs?

This chapter explores the church's ministries of providing child care and weekday educational programs. Various types of programs, special concerns, and the role of church committees will be considered, but it is important first to understand the impetus for these endeavors.

- Because Jesus welcomed children.

  As followers of Jesus, we welcome children in Jesus' name. The church I attend has just completed a yearlong celebration of children in the church. In keeping with the Presbyterian Church (U.S.A.)'s vision statement for children's ministries,[1] congregations express concern for children by providing quality child care and weekday education that not only nurtures the children of our congregations but also addresses the needs of children in our broader communities.

- Because Jesus held up a child as an example of how we are to receive the realm (or kingdom) of God.

  In the midst of a culture that says, "Hurry up, grow up, become like adults as soon as possible," we, as disciples of Jesus, are called to value childhood and childlikeness by planning programs that honor the right of children to be children and by celebrating the special aspects of childhood. By providing safe, caring environments in which play, wonder, and imagination are treated as gifts to be celebrated, we become advocates of childlikeness and lay the foundation for spiritual development in children.

- Because of the vows that the congregation takes at the time of baptism.

  When children are baptized, congregations promise to nurture them in the faith. Church members then become like godparents to those baptized, providing support to parents in the demanding task of Christian nurture. Programs of child care and education in the church may be regarded as manifestations of this partnership with parents, providing children with windows to God and comprising a key component of family ministries.

Types of Programs

Most churches provide church school for all ages and nursery care for young children. Practicing partnership with parents in raising young children in the faith, however, can include a wide spectrum of activities. Nursery care can be extended to allow parents to participate in worship and in congregational meetings, Bible studies, choir, and other important activities with the knowledge that their children will have loving, responsive care in safe, secure facilities. Since many churches have spaces designed for children, it makes sense to utilize these facilities for more than Sunday morning.

Listed below are some possible programs. Consider how each might meet the needs of parents in your congregation, the needs of your broader community, and the need for your church membership to be faithful stewards of the church facility.

- Parents' Morning or Day Out

  Offered once or twice a week, this ministry allows stay-at-home parents to have adult time or an opportunity to engage in activities without having children along.

- Parents' Night Out

  This ministry gives parents two or three hours on Friday or Saturday evening to enjoy a dinner, movie, or other date to strengthen their marital partnership.

- Weekday Programs

  These include preschool classes, toddler play groups, and part- or full-day child-care programs for working parents. Other weekday programs may serve special populations of children in the community, such as children with physical or mental disabilities; children with emotional or mental health needs; children who have been abused; children who need to learn English; or children who need tutorial programs or experience with computers.

- Summer Programs

These include vacation Bible school, day camps, art enrichment programs, and special tutoring.

If your facilities are not adequate for some of the programs mentioned above, you might consider organizing a family day-care network of home-based providers who could be trained at or have a resource center of educational materials in your church building. Additional child-care support can be provided by setting up a babysitting co-op among parents in the church or by keeping a list of babysitters who have been trained to work as volunteers in the church nursery.

Special Concerns for Weekday Programs

There are several issues that church governing boards and committees need to address regarding weekday programs that are housed in church buildings. These are mission, governance, administration, finances, and liaison between the weekday program and the other regular programs taking place in the church facilities.[2] Each of these issues may be related to one or more committees of the congregation as well as to the church's governing board.

Mission

Of critical importance is the mission statement of the weekday program. The mission statement influences governance, curriculum, admission guidelines, personnel policies, and relationship to the congregation's overall mission. The mission statement answers questions such as: What population is being served? What are the goals of the program? Is the primary purpose to provide Christian education, to offer support systems for members of the congregation, to engage in community service, to minister to a particular population, or to attract new families to the church? How does the weekday program relate to the overall mission of the church? The answer to the last question deeply affects the structural connection between the children's program and the organizational pattern of the church. The mission statement also helps determine which church committee will have primary oversight of the program. It is interesting to note that in a National Council of Church's Study of Child Care in the

1980s,[3] mission statements were aimed at community service, social justice, and stewardship of facilities, while program goals included sharing and cooperation, positive self-image, values of love and worth, or general moral and religious values. A more recent study[4] indicates that religious education, the spiritual development of children, and evangelism are more prominent goals of weekday programming.

Governance

Questions of governance, responsibility, and liability flow from the mission statement of weekday children's program. Three basic organizational patterns for children's programs in churches have been identified.[5] These are church-housed, church-sponsored, and church-operated.

- Church-housed programs are independently operated in rented church space. Issues of liability, insurance, and conditions of shared space need to be carefully delineated in the written rental agreement. It is also important to consider the program's philosophy when deciding whether or not to rent church property because parents may assume that since the program is held on church property, the children will be well cared for in accord with the church's beliefs and value system. It would be wise to seek input from insurance and legal professionals when considering renting church space for a weekday children's program.

- Church-sponsored programs are akin to parochial schools in which the program is incorporated separately for liability and funding purposes, has its own governing board, and enters into a contractual agreement with the church. The church is involved through representation on program's governing board.

- Church-operated programs, which are directly operated by the church under the governing board's jurisdiction, are becoming increasingly popular. These programs may function under a committee (e.g., education/nurture or mission) representing the ministry area most closely related to the program's mission statement and goals. In other cases, a special board or committee may be appointed by the governing board. This committee would include representation not only from Christian education but also from other committees such as the property committee, along with persons with pertinent expertise in areas such as law, funding, health or social services, and child advocacy; and, of course, the committee should include parents.

Administration

Closely related to governance, administration deals with accountability between the congregation and child-care program in matters of liability, safety, health and legal requirements, personnel policies, child abuse reporting and prevention policies, and other issues related to the day-to-day operation of the center or school. The key person is the director of the weekday program. An important administrative issue is designating to whom the weekday program director is accountable in the operation of the program. Possibilities include the head of staff, the director of Christian education or minister of education, and the chair of the appropriate committee. The director of the weekday program, along with designated congregational leaders, provides an annual review of licensing, liability, employee practices, and other legal requirements, as well as personnel policies, program goals, status of facilities, discipline policies, fiscal and financial practices, and procedures. Designated congregational leaders may come from finance, personnel, or property committees of the church in addition to the committee or ministry area to which the program is directly accountable. It is important that the bylaws, personnel, admissions, and operating policies be reviewed annually by persons designated by the church's governing board. The education committee needs to review program goals, curriculum, staff-child ratios, physical environment, discipline policies, and other educational concerns.

If the children's weekday program is included in the church's overall ministry, then program staff are considered members of the church staff and entitled to benefits such as health coverage, retirement, parking, office space and support, and continuing education. This is a neglected area in many church weekday programs where frequently low wages and lack of benefits mean that the staff essentially subsidizes the care and education of children. This may allow churches to provide lower cost child care and education than other providers, but a study by Mary Bogle of religious-based child care[6] found it to be of lower quality than other programs because of lack of support and training for teachers and caregivers. Recognition of teachers and caregivers in weekday programs is essential. Public acknowledgment on teacher dedication/commissioning Sunday and inclusion in teacher-appreciation activities are ways to honor those who teach and care for children on a daily basis.

Finances

Mutual accountability between the church and its weekday children's programs includes the area of finance. Where does fiscal responsibility lie? Although it lies with the board in separately incorporated centers and schools, the sponsoring church is represented on the board. In church-operated centers the church is ultimately responsible. Some churches have thought of children's weekday programs as moneymakers. Although it may be good stewardship to utilize space designed for children for more than church school, a short vacation Bible school, or a one evening a week program, a weekday child-care center or preschool may also help share expenses for utilities and janitorial services. Many churches donate these services as in-kind contributions to the weekday program's budget to subsidize quality early childhood programs, making costs more reasonable for parents.

In order to assist low-income parents, some churches that run weekday children's programs offer sliding-scale tuition fees.[7] This financial structure assures a socioeconomic mix to the population served. The social dimensions of this structure provide children opportunities for wider experience and exposure to economic diversity—a value supported by early childhood educators. This kind of subsidy from the church may be considered part of the local mission budget.

Groups in the church may be encouraged to make special gifts (perhaps memorial gifts) to scholarship funds for families of children in the center who suffer temporary financial reversals such as a parental layoff or medical emergencies. It is best for children to remain in the stable environment of the weekday program. Both a sliding-scale tuition structure and an emergency fund assist in church programs that depend on tuition as the major source of funding.

Public funding for faith-based community projects like child care may be explored in terms of tuition vouchers or direct grants to church programs. Congregations exploring these funding initiatives need to study the church/state issues involved in curriculum and personnel standards dictated by adherence to national guidelines from the early childhood profession. For programs with a strong religious education component, receiving federal monies with accompanying educational standards may be problematic.

In some churches, the financial management, fee collection, and fund disbursement is handled by the church's business office. In others, the finances of weekday programs are managed by the director of the program or the board treasurer. In all cases, those in charge of the church's finances need to have budget reviews and/or audits of the program's finances to assure that appropriate procedures are followed.

Liaison

Weekday program staff often feels unsupported and sees their work as detached from the church's ongoing ministry. Additionally, the use of shared space can create a "we/they" tension between church school teachers and weekday program staff. A strong relationship is necessary, therefore, between congregations and the weekday program staff and board.

The demands of rearranging the space on Friday afternoon and Monday morning to accommodate the shifts between the weekday program and Sunday school takes a toll on both sets of teachers. Written agreements and open communication can help bridge any we/they conflicts. Separate storage space for each group can help to ease tensions in the multiple use of rooms, equipment, and resources, although sharing is ideal. The role of the church educator in working with both groups can help ease tensions. The pamphlet "Fifty Nifty Ideas," circulated by the Ecumenical Child Care Network, is a helpful tool.[8]

Written covenants[9] that spell out the mutual responsibilities of both the church and weekday programs are necessary for enhancing a sense of connection between programs. Covenants should be reviewed annually and carefully interpreted to all involved parties. The written covenant needs to include not only the conditions of shared space and facilities, but also in-kind contributions of utilities, janitorial service, maintenance and replacement of equipment; office usage and support; persons to notify in emergency situations; procedures of fire safety and evacuations in crisis situations; food service collaboration; rules for using outdoor space and equipment; and anything else that supports the liaison between the church and its programs for children.

Additional opportunities for strengthening connections and sharing resources can be found in teacher training, parent education, newsletter coverage and displays, moments for mission, and hosting open houses. In many churches, congregational volunteers enrich the children's weekday programs by reading stories, fixing toys and equipment, or engaging in activities like gardening or cooking with the children. Groups within the congregation can provide volunteer staffing during nap time to give teachers planning or staff development time. In one church, a women's group provides holiday snacks for child-care staff lounges or hosts an annual appreciation luncheon for teachers.

Just as it takes a whole village to raise a child, it takes the whole congregation to mount and sustain the operation of an extensive ministry with children in the church and community. It is clear from the preceding discussion of church-housed programs for young children that many areas of ministry are involved. The following section offers suggestions of how various committees of the church can be involved in the comprehensive care and education of children.

Suggestions for Committee Involvement

The Worship Committee

- Provide quality child care during regular and special services
- Provide quality child care during adult choir practice
- Provide music education for children
- Work with the Christian education committee to conduct children's activities during and related to preparation for inclusion in worship

The Budget and Finance Committee

- Provide equipment and staff (many churches provide paid staff who work alongside volunteers in order to ensure continuity for nursery care)
- Oversee funding and financial operation of weekday programs

The Personnel Committee

- Ensure adequate staff salaries and benefits for child caregivers and teachers
- Support professional development of staff
- Designate staff supervision and evaluate performance
- Approve hiring and firing procedures

The Membership Committee

- Recruit newcomers for church membership from those attending weekday programs
- Support assimilation of families with young children into the church's programs
- Conduct needs assessment for additional children's programs

The Property or Building and Grounds Committee

- Attend to safety and health requirements of facilities
- Provide for emergency or evacuation plans

- Maintain facilities and equipment according to state licensing standards[10]
- Set conditions and supervise arrangements for sharing classrooms, kitchen, offices, playground, fellowship hall, and storage areas
- Provide child-sized restrooms, water fountains, water for activities, appropriate child-level display areas, and so on

The Mission and Outreach Committee

- Explore needs and services for children in the community
- Collaborate with larger churches, ecumenical groups, and public agencies in meeting the needs of children
- Advocate for children's services
- Make suggestions for how congregational resources can be utilized in serving particular populations of children
- Monitor mission statements of children's programs in light of the congregation's mission priorities

The Christian Education (Nurture) Committee

- Set up a children's ministries subcommittee to monitor programs for adequate space, teacher/child ratio, use of appropriate equipment, educational materials, curriculum, and discipline policies
- Provide consultation and oversight of shared educational space provisions
- Provide training for developmentally appropriate teaching
- Promote values and dimensions of spiritual development where appropriate
- Suggest joint efforts in parent education

The Publicity or Interpretation Committee

- Publicize children's programs on church Web site, in church newsletter, and in local newspapers
- Display children's art and photos of programs
- Invite the weekday program director to speak to groups in the congregation

The Long-Range and Strategic Planning Committee

- Include children's ministries when setting priorities and goals for congregational emphases

- Monitor weekday program's mission statement in light of congregational mission
- Explore possible joint ventures with other churches or agencies in community if the church cannot independently support certain children's programs

NOTES

1. The vision statement can be found in Mary Anne Fowlkes, *The Church Cares for Children* (Louisville: Curriculum Publishing Program Area, 1995, p. 11), or *The Mission Yearbook for Prayer and Study*, (Louisville, KY: Congregational Ministries Publishing, Presbyterian Church U.S.A., 2000).

2. Adapted from D. M. Steele, ed. *Congregations and Child Care: A Self Study for Churches and Synagogues and Their Early Childhood Programs* (New York: National Council of Churches of Christ in the U.S.A., 1996). Prepared by the Ecumenical Child Care Network in cooperation with the National Association for the Education of Young Children for accreditation of church-based child-care centers by the National Academy of Early Childhood Programs.

3. E. W. Lindner, Mary C. Mattis, J. R. Rogers, *When Churches Mind the Children: A Study of Daycare in Local Parishes* (Ypsilanti, MI: High/Scope Press, 1983).

4. Mary Bogle, *The Involvement of Religious Congregations in Early Care and Education in the U.S.* Paper prepared for the Brookings Institution (1775 Massachusetts Ave. NW, Washington, DC 20036-2188 (202) 797-6000), March 14, 2001.

5. Margery Freeman, ed., *Helping Churches Mind the Children: A Guide for Church-Housed Child Care Programs* (New York: National Council of Churches of Christ in the U.S.A., 1987), p. 17.

6. Bogle, p. 19.

7. For helpful discussions of sliding fees, scholarship support, and general information on funding for low-income families, see "Ecumenical Child Care Newsletter," vol. VI (6), November/December 1988 (9765 West Higgins Rd., Suite 405, Chicago, IL 60631 (800) 649-5443).

8. Included in Mary Anne Fowlkes, *The Church Cares for Children* (Louisville, KY: Curriculum Publishing Program Area, 1995), p. 59.

9. A sample covenant agreement can be found in *Helping Churches Mind the Children* (New York: National Council of Churches of Christ in the U.S.A., 1987), p. 50.

10. Church education space for children needs to meet the child-care licensing standards for your state. Even if church-housed programs have a religious exemption in your state, most church educational space should meet the health and safety standards required for children's programs as a dimension of providing quality care for God's children.

RESOURCES

Bogle, Mary. *The Involvement of Religious Congregations in Early Care and Education in the U.S.* Paper prepared for the Brookings Institution, 1775 Massachusetts Ave. NW, Washington, DC 20036-2188, (202) 797-6000, March 14, 2001. Provides information on public funding for child care in faith-based communities and guidance in church/state relationships.

Fowlkes, Mary Anne. *The Church Cares for Children.* Louisville, KY: Curriculum Publishing Program Area, 1995.

Margery Freeman, ed., *Helping Churches Mind the Children: A Guide for Church-Housed Child Care Programs.* New York, NY: National Council of Churches of Christ in the U.S.A., 1987. Revised version available through Ecumenical Child Care Network, 9765 West Higgins Rd., Suite 405, Chicago, IL 60631, (800) 649–5443. A valuable resource for starting programs.

Smith, Susan Keil, and Lois Rifner. "We Won't Let It Happen Here! Preventing Child Sexual Abuse in the Church," in *Striking Terror No More: The Church Responds to Domestic Violence.* Edited by Beth Basham and Sara Lisherness. Louisville, KY: Bridge Resources, 1997.

CHAPTER SEVEN

Children and the Work
of Church Committees

The Work of the Christian Education Committee

Joyce MacKichan Walker

"I love committee meetings!" Did you ever think you'd hear that? I am never surprised to hear it. I have known many people who love committee meetings for many reasons! The child care committee that meets at my church has a very regular meeting night plan: open with prayer, go through five to six pages of the sorted-by-birthdate list of all the children in our church from birth through age two; review the parents who participate in the "co-op" and those who don't; remove the names of those families who have moved or no longer attend the church; and go out for coffee and dessert. The timing goes like this: thirty minutes for items one through four, one to two hours for item five. The last time we met, the pastor stuck his head inside the door and asked, "Is this the committee that meets for ten minutes and drinks coffee for an hour?" We all nodded our heads and smiled.

"I hate committee meetings!" Did you ever think you'd hear that? I am never surprised to hear it. I have known many people who hate committee meetings for many reasons! "We don't *do* anything worthwhile!" "We just talk, we don't do anything!" "The moderator has an agenda, moves through it, makes assignments, and gets us out of there—we never get to talk!" "Everyone sits around with their eyes down so they won't get a job!" "We do the same things every year—it works fine but it's always the same old thing!" "There are so many administrative tasks—it takes all night to deal with the details!" "I need a place to be involved that feeds me!" I suspect you have heard these complaints and more.

Committees are important. Find a church that consistently provides thriving, quality programs and someplace behind it you will find hard-working, committed, caring committee members. What makes it all work? A more important question is, "How can *your* church make it work?" Wait—perhaps the *most* important question is, "How can your church make it fun, engaging, fulfilling, and worthwhile?"

A book could be written on the role and work of a children's education committee. For the purposes of this presentation, we will focus on five actions that address not only traditional organizational and administrative issues, but also offer support for a comprehensive ministry in which children are cared for and their place in the community of faith is emphasized. These five actions are: *attend* to the faith lives of committee members; *involve* the committee in shaping and evaluating its mission; *organize* for effective and efficient work together; *claim* a place within the whole ministry of the church; and *challenge* committee members to expand their understandings of faith and of children.

Attend to the Faith Lives of Committee Members

It is important for committee members to take time to remember whose they are and why they do what they do for the community of faith. This may require something as simple as beginning and ending committee work with prayer, but more often, it takes deliberate attention to committee members and their ministry. Below are some ways to claim Christian identity, nurture spirituality, and make committee work become ministry.

- Shape interactive times of prayer and reflection to honor committee members' lives of faith and enhance awareness of the community they serve. *Meeting God in the Bible: Sixty Devotions for Groups*[1] has everything you will need for this endeavor.
- Engage in classic spiritual practices by using one to begin each meeting or choosing one to focus on for several months. *Spirit Windows: A Handbook of Spiritual Growth Resources for Leaders* by Ann Z. Kulp[2] is a good resource for exploring spiritual practices.

- Develop your own questions from the two basic questions of the spiritual practice called "the examen." These questions are, "What gave you life this day?" and "What drained life from you this day?" Relate the questions to the work of the committee and allow the responses to shape the committee's work toward those things that bring life. You can learn more about the practice of examen from *Sleeping with Bread: Holding What Gives You Life*.[3]

- Offer thanksgiving for each joy expressed during committee meetings and offer prayers of petition for each concern. At the beginning of a meeting, invite one person to list the joys named during the time together and another person to note the concerns. End the meeting by having each list read one item at a time, using the respective responses, "Thank you, God," and "Hear our prayer."

- Look to the psalms for guidance in ministry with children. At the first meeting of the year, provide a list of psalms that offer insight into the nature of the God who calls us to minister to children and the congregation. Psalm 1; 8; 16; 19; 23; 24; 29; 43:3-5; 46; 61:1–5, 8; 65; 67; 77; 84; 93; 96; 98; 99; 100; 103; 113; 121; 131; 133; 134; 135; 136; 138; 139:1–18, 23–24; 145; 146; 148; and 150 are good choices. Invite committee members to select one psalm and one meeting date on which to read the psalm as the opening prayer.

- Dedicate the first part of each meeting to praying specifically for one church school class. Read the names of the children in the class, name the teachers, briefly recall what the class is studying, and pray for their experience.

Involve the Committee in Shaping and Evaluating Its Mission

Once a year is not too often to review the charter for a committee's work. If you don't have a charter and operate on the basis of doing what needs to be done, it's time to create one. Rather than letting a pastor or governing board create the charter, engage the committee in defining its own work. Reflect on such questions as: Who are the children we serve? What is the church called to be for these children? What are our goals for our work together? What do we want children to learn? What do we want children to encounter in this place? What do we believe God calls them to be and do? Who can best help us do our work? What gifts and skills are needed to do our work? Such reflection will help lay the foundation for the charter.

Creating a simple mission statement is a stimulating and energizing exercise. A very simple and effective model for creating a mission statement can be found in *The Path: Creating Your Mission Statement for Work and for Life*,[4] which offers a very clear handout of a step-by-step process of identifying an audience, a core value, and three action verbs. Following the process results in a brief mission statement that helps to focus a committee on its most important charge. The mission statements that follow were written by children's education committees in forty-five minutes.

- The mission of the children's education committee is to foster, inspire, and innovate for the faith of the children of the community.
- The mission of the children's education committee is to plant (engage), water (empower), and grow (nurture) faith in our children and their parents.

It is important to put the mission statement in conspicuous places where it can invite conversation, encourage honest and open reflection, and inspire action. Revisiting the charter periodically will remind committee members what is important, prompt the evaluation of current work, and allow the committee to identify steps for fuller achievement of its mission. Below are steps created by one children's education committee.

- provide a nurturing and safe environment
- provide resources, including the names of faithful people with special skills
- involve the children's parents
- intentionally develop children's spirituality
- develop ways to connect what is happening in church school classrooms to homes
- involve children in their own learning
- ask for more adult education offerings for parents on matters that affect their children (parenting skills, dealing with tough questions of faith, nurturing faith at home)
- connect our work to the work of other committees in the church for an integrated approach to faith development and to the whole ministry of the church

- provide opportunities to serve at every age

- connect what is happening in educational settings to our lives of faith as disciples of Jesus Christ

Organize for Effective and Efficient Work Together

A routine enhances committee work and helps focus energy on important tasks for ministry to children and the church. The most effective tool I have found for directing a committee's work is a simple monthly calendar of regular tasks. Organizing the tasks in a twelve-block chart provides visual reinforcement of the cyclical nature of these important aspects of ministry.

To create a monthly calendar, begin by listing the regular tasks and commitments of the committee and placing them in the month(s) in which they need attention. The easiest way to generate this list is to review past minutes, noting those things that appear regularly. The next step is to identify those that need to be addressed each year but require no particular time slot, such as reflection on the committee's mission statement, evaluation of overall programs, identification of new challenges, communication, and new visions for ministry. These tasks can be placed on the calendar in slots where there will be sufficient time to adequately address them. It is important to leave room in each month's square for unanticipated responsibilities that require immediate attention.

A sample calendar is provided below. This sample reflects the work of a separate children's education committee serving a large church. Smaller churches administer educational ministry for all ages under one committee. A calendar for a small church would contain some different items and possibly fewer tasks related to children's ministry.

January

- Hold Christian education retreat[5] to welcome new members, evaluate the past year, and envision new ministries (may include all teachers and midweek leaders, and all education committees if the church has age-group committees)

February

- Plan teacher appreciation for Easter
- Discuss curriculum resources for next year
- Set up a vacation Bible school planning committee
- Review plan for summer education activities and staffing

March

- Begin process of staffing church school classes and midweek programs for the next year (check with current teachers and substitutes)
- Review process of finding new teachers; extend invitations
- Promote church camping programs and early registration

April

- Continue the process of inviting new teachers and leaders to serve
- Plan a closing event for the church school and midweek programs
- Plan teacher and leader appreciation for end of year

May

- Continue inviting new teachers and leaders
- Begin plans for teacher workshops for the fall and leadership training events
- Walk the building—note major room, furniture, and equipment needs; submit requests

June

- Evaluate this year's response to children with special needs and plan placements for the next year
- Review the year—make notes about revisions and changes
- Project the class sizes and rooms
- Schedule room and supply-closet cleaning over the summer
- Review procedures for inviting, welcoming, and including new children and families

July

- Order programming supplies, fall curriculum resources (schedule regularly as needed)
- Determine special events for the coming year (such as gift of Bibles to a class, preparation for children's participation in the sacrament of the Lord's Supper, church-year emphases, all church or all church school mission projects, all-ages activities)
- Plan a beginning of the church school celebration, registration procedures, and installation of teachers
- Plan communication to families and the whole church about fall opportunities

August
- You're ready—take a break!
  or

- Finalize church school leadership team
- Host beginning of the year activities
- Plan a systematic check-in with classes and teachers in the first two weeks of church school

September
- Host beginning of the year activities
- Check on teacher support systems
- Make plans for Advent worship and activities
- Review current budget and needs and prepare budget proposal for the coming year

October
- No meeting—things are going smoothly and according to plan
  or

- Evaluate major programs, church school and midweek program start-up, communications systems, and child protection policies and procedures
- Consider new needs that have arisen

November
- Begin planning for Lent and Easter activities
- Plan teacher appreciation for Christmas season
- Plan teacher education workshops for late winter

December
- No meeting: celebrate Advent and Christmas with your family and loved ones

Claim a Place within the Whole Ministry of the Church

Children are a part of the faith community. They are called to worship God, serve as disciples of Jesus Christ, invite others to follow Jesus, welcome others into the community of faith, learn, and grow as they live lives of wonder, questioning, experimenting, and exploring their faith. In order for children to participate fully in the ministries of the congregation, it is important for the Christian education committee to remember it plans not just formal educational events for children but for their full participation in the body of Jesus

Christ. Below are suggestions for how your church might actively welcome children into full participation.

- Consider how children can participate in every mission effort the church plans or supports. For example, children can collect items or money, lend their hands in work, write letters, draw pictures, make cards, extend encouragement, create a cheer, send notes, bring and serve lemonade, bake cookies or bread, make welcome home signs, invite mission participants to tell their stories, write a prayer, and pray for participants by name. Nothing the church does, big or small, near or far away, need exclude the children from participating in some way.
- Be intentional about having church leaders—elders, deacons, pastors, trustees, committee members, custodians, and organization officers—meet with children and describe their ministries.
- Give children their own stewardship envelopes, either for church school or worship. Inform children how the church spends the money that people give so they know where their offerings go and who they are helping.
- Include children as worship leaders whenever possible: on special occasions, in all church school worship experiences, and in classroom and midweek programming.
- Encourage pastors and leaders to include children in their prayers; to refer to children as ministers and disciples; to invite children to serve as ushers, greeters, and those who receive and present the offering.
- Work cooperatively with choir directors to ensure that children's musical talents are encouraged and developed. The best music programs for children are designed to teach the stories of the faith through music, to furnish children with a faith vocabulary that feeds them for a lifetime, and to provide children with the opportunity to help lead worship as members of a children's choir.

Challenge Committee Members to Expand Their Understandings of Faith and of Children

This look at the work of the Christian education committee began with consideration of ways to feed the spiritual lives of committee members. Inviting committee members to become knowledgeable advocates for children and providing resources for that quest will take their leadership to a higher level. During the Year of the Child, the moderator of the General Assembly of the PC(USA) for 1998–1999, Douglas Oldenburg, challenged every church to engage in a project on behalf of the world's children. Caring for your own is not enough. God calls us to be for all God's children—and surely children's education committees have a particular responsibility to care, act, and lead in this regard. Below is a list of some resources and ideas for fulfilling this broader calling on behalf of children.

- *Practicing Our Faith: A Way of Life for a Searching People*[6] introduces twelve faith practices or "things Christian people do together over time in response to and in the light of God's active presence for the life of the world." In addition to stimulating faith-shaping conversations among adult committee members, a careful exploration of some of these practices could be used to devise plans for the development of faith practices for children.
- Many denominations have free periodicals for teachers and leaders in Christian education. The Presbyterian Church (U.S.A.) publishes *Ideas! For Church Leaders*, a quarterly publication of Congregational Ministries Publishing/Marketing. For more information, visit the denominational Web site at www.pcusa.org/ideas.
- Books abound about children and children's development, connecting church and home and enhancing educational ministry. See the resource list at the end of this section for titles that will feed the minds, hearts, and energy levels of Christian education committees. Ongoing conversation about the children we serve and about ways to teach for faith keep committee meetings lively and committee members mindful of the importance of their work together.

Taking responsibility for a congregation's ministry to, for, and with children is an extraordinary task. When Jesus said, "Let the little children come to me; do not stop them; for it is to such as these that the kingdom of God belongs" (Mark 10:14b), he followed his words with an action that made tangible the enfolding love of God: "And he took them up in his arms, laid his hands on them, and blessed them" (Mark 10:6). As people called out of a congregation to minister to God's children, in the halls and classrooms of our churches and *wherever* children may be, we take on the responsibility for literally and figuratively enfolding them in God's love. May our efforts on behalf of children also be a blessing of time spent in ministry together and a blessing for the entire congregation that supports these ministries and in turn receives those blessings uniquely offered by children.

NOTES

1. Donald L. Griggs (Pittsburgh: Kerygma Program, 1992).
2. Ann Z. Kulp (Louisville: Witherspoon Press, 1997).
3. Dennis Linn et al., (New York: Paulist Press, 1995).
4. Laurie Beth Jones (New York: Hyperion, 1996).
5. This yearly morning or day-long retreat can be very important to a congregation's educational program. A significant block of time scheduled outside of regular committee meetings allows the freedom to think creatively about the overall picture. Without it, it is easy to get caught up in regular tasks and neglect the evaluation, reflection, and visioning that keep programming in tune with a changing world and, very possibly, a changing congregation. Possible topics for exploration include new program ideas, who the congregation serves, a congregational self-study, life-changing learning, and special all-church educational events.
6. Dorothy C. Bass (San Francisco: Jossey-Bass, 1997)

RESOURCES

Dorothy C. Bass, ed. *Practicing Our Faith*. San Francisco: Jossey-Bass, 1997.

Caldwell, Elizabeth. *Making a Home for Faith*. Cleveland: United Church Press, 2000.

Cloyd, Betty. *Children and Prayer: A Shared Pilgrimage*. Nashville: Upper Room Press, 1997.

Coles, Robert. *The Spiritual Life of Children*. Boston: Houghton Mifflin, 1990.

Foster, Charles. *Educating Congregations: The Future of Christian Education*. Nashville: Abingdon Press, 1994.

Griggs, Donald L. *Meeting God in the Bible: Sixty Devotions for Groups*. Pittsburgh: Kerygma Program, 1992.

Juengst, Sara Covin. *Equipping the Saints: Teacher Training in the Church*. Louisville, KY: Westminster John Knox Press, 1998.

Kulp, Ann Z. *Spirit Windows: A Handbook of Spiritual Growth Resources for Leaders*. Louisville, KY: Bridge Resources, 1998.

Linn, Dennis, Sheila Fabricant Linn, and Matthew Linn. *Sleeping with Bread: Holding What Gives You Life*. New York: Paulist Press, 1995.

Sinclair, Donna, and Yvonne Stewart. *Christian Parenting: Raising Children in the Real World*. Louisville, KY: Westminster John Knox Press, 1992.

Webb-Mitchell, Brett. *Dancing with Disabilities: Opening the Church to All God's Children*. Cleveland: United Church Press, 1996.

Worship: The Work of Everyone

Jean Floyd Love

Worship is the central act of a gathered community of the people of God, and, as the Directory for Worship states, "the work of everyone" (W-1.4003). This "work" involves singing, praising, praying, touching, listening, giving, and departing to serve. Worship is central to faith and "everyone" includes children. Children, by virtue of being baptized, are members of the family of God. They belong to the fellowship as persons loved by God. They are to be respected as persons. They are valued for who they are and not for the adults they will become. As church family members, children need to be included in worship from an early age.

> Children of any age can worship. They may not worship in the same way or at the same cognitive level as adults, but they still worship. Fortunately, being a Christian is not entirely a cognitive matter. It is also a matter of affections, symbols, story, and mystery. Most of us became Christians not by thinking about the faith and making rational decisions about Christ, but rather by watching our elders and then growing into faith in a natural way, the way we inherited most of our important values.[1]

Worship, then, is also one of the means by which the church passes on its beliefs and practices. Children and youth *participate* their way into faith. They form their identities as Christians unconsciously, through the liturgy (work) of the worship in which they participate. Understanding starts at the level of impression and awareness, and experience precedes rational understanding, so children are learning whether or not they are able to verbalize that learning. Children learn the feelings, postures, gestures, attitudes, and words of worship by observing and imitating adults. As with all spiritual disciplines, worship takes practice—a great deal of practice. Children will learn to worship and to value worship by participating in the worship experience on a regular basis. *Children learn to worship by worshiping.*

The primary responsibility for seeing that children are included in worship rests with the pastor and the church's governing body.

> In setting an order for worship on the Lord's Day, the pastor with the concurrence of the session shall provide opportunity for the people from youngest to oldest to participate in a worthy offering of praise to God and for them to hear and to respond to God's Word (Directory for Worship, W-3.3201).

The central occasion for nurture in the church is the Service for the Lord's Day, when the Word is proclaimed and the Sacraments are celebrated. All members of the community, from oldest to youngest, are encouraged to be present and to participate. Educational activities should not be scheduled which prevent regular participation in this service (Directory for Worship, W-6.2006). Beyond these reasons for including children in worship is the contribution that children make to the community's worship experience.

> Children bring special gifts to worship and grow in the faith through their regular inclusion and participation in the worship of the congregation. Those responsible for planning and leading the participation of children in worship should consider the children's level of understanding and ability to respond, and should avoid both excessive formality and condescension (Directory for Worship, W-3.1004).

Children indeed have unique gifts to offer the receptive congregation. These include:

- a reminder of the vows adults make during the sacrament of baptism
- a spontaneity that provokes smiles, demands flexibility, and adds spice to community life
- an ability to see things as they really are
- an alternative (other than adult) view of the world
- an openness to God and a freshness in celebrating God's love
- a propensity for using all the senses and a model for multisensory worship
- unhesitating faith
- a willingness to ask questions that make all of us think seriously about faith
- their presence, especially for those who do not have children in their daily lives
- vulnerability
- challenges to established beliefs, activities, and models of living out the faith
- genuine smiles

Ways to Include Children in Congregational Worship

Among the ways to include children in congregational worship are those in which they can actively participate, such as to:

- serve as greeter with an adult partner
- hand out children's bulletins or other items to be used in worship
- serve as an acolyte
- carry in the Bible during the procession
- sing in the children's choir
- help teach the congregation a new hymn or movements to a familiar song
- carry in the communion bread
- interpret a call to worship, Scripture reading, or song through movement
- read Scripture
- compose a litany
- lead a litany
- participate in the moment with children
- design bulletin covers
- bring in an offering of canned goods for hunger relief or other items for disaster relief
- play a musical instrument
- participate in the passing of the peace
- make and present a banner
- make and/or present a gift to parents of a newly baptized baby
- make a tablecloth for the Communion table
- take up the offering

For many congregations, the moment with children or children's sermon is the primary way that children are included in congregation. This practice has come under scrutiny in recent years. Below is a partial list of the positive and negative aspects of having children's sermons.

The Children's Sermon: The Positive Side

- provides an opportunity to affirm, in a variety of ways, children's importance to God
- helps integrate children into the ritual life of the community
- provides the opportunity for proclamation in age-appropriate language
- reminds adults that they, too, are dependent children of a loving God
- provides a visual reminder to the congregation of its responsibility to children
- when delivered by the pastor, affirms the pastor's care for and interest in children

- provides tangible expression of the willingness of the adult leaders to meet the children at their level of understanding
- transmits the traditions and values of the community

The Children's Sermon: The Negative Side

- while conveying the important place children hold in the church, it may also suggest to children that they are not like the rest of the congregation

    Any process within the context of worship that singles out a particular group for special recognition or attention endangers the ability to remain an intentionally inclusive and whole community.[2]

- does little to assist children in getting through the remainder of an adult-focused service
- provides time for children to have the full attention of the pastor, but many pastors are not comfortable in this setting
- provides a poor substitute for a relationship with the pastor and integration into community life[3]
- often more appreciated by adults as "entertainment" than by children, who can sense when they are being used; instead they should be treated with respect, and never exploited, manipulated, or patronized
- contains messages often too abstract for children to understand and not related to children's experiences; for example, the ever popular "object lesson" generally requires the children to make a mental leap from the concrete object to an abstract concept, which is a cognitive function that younger children have not yet developed
- implies that the other sermon and the rest of worship are relevant only for adults

    Worship is more than preaching. Scripture is read, heard, responded to, sung, prayed, acted out, shared, and experienced by persons in different ways. It is important is remember that "enthusiasm in worship, overt expressions of moods, treatment of others, postures and gestures in worship, and even the preaching event . . . are observable and can be imitated."[4]

Scripture Reading, Preaching, and Children

Sermon time is the most problematic time for parents and children. Whatever is done to encourage children will also assist worshipers of all ages. Below are listed suggestions for helping children hear Scripture readings and sermons.[5]

Scripture readings

- offer a prayer for illumination prior to reading
- establish the context for the passage prior to reading, setting the scene and inviting listeners into it
- have members of the congregation, including children, serve as liturgists
- read Scripture as a litany
- read the passage so as to convey its dramatic or emotional character
- engage several voices when the passage has more than one character
- read from a translation that most clearly presents the Scripture selection
- show an object that is featured in the text such as a plumb line or potter's clay

Sermons

- use props or familiar objects when appropriate
- define and illustrate "big words"
- guide the listeners by indicating ways to follow the sermon and summarizing frequently
- use questions, illustrations, and examples from the lives of children and youth as well as adults
- present some insights from a child's viewpoint
- become familiar with children's literature, music, and films and when appropriate include them in the sermon
- address children from time to time
- use images, metaphors, and analogies
- use humor appropriately
- strive for seventeen-minute sermons
- remember that the need to shift in the pew is not age-specific[6]

Worship is enriched for all when the use of all the senses is increased and the body is actively engaged. Children teach us that when we get stuck in one medium, such as the spoken word, attention drifts. A mix of focal points, movement, music, and symbols will help all worshipers to focus on the object of our worship—God. It is important to admit that adults rarely get through a full-length liturgy without lapses in attention. Adults become inattentive from time to time, staring into space, leafing through the bulletin, mentally (or physically) making a list of things to be done, or closing our eyes for a while. Children have not yet learned such socially acceptable ways of checking out, so they express their inattention more noticeably.

Barriers to Full Participation of Children in Worship

There are a number of practices and perspectives that prevent children's full participation in congregational worship. Many of these are unconscious and, once noted, can be adjusted to the benefit of children and the entire congregation. Below is a list of common barriers to children's full participation in worship.

- scheduling worship and education simultaneously—regardless of the reasons, the result is that adults worship, children attend church school, and neither receives the full experience of worship and education; each group is also deprived of the gifts, insights, and wisdom the others have to share
- viewing worship as entertainment and the worship leaders as performers
- failing to educate the worshipers (all ages) about what worship is and how expectations shape the worship experience
- assuming that children are so different from adults that they cannot "get" anything from the worship experience
- presuming that it is too difficult to preach effectively to the wide range of ages represented by the gathered community
- neglecting parenting responsibilities during worship—this is an important time for parents to help children learn to worship and experience the presence of God (which goes beyond admonitions to sit still and includes helping with hymnbooks and encouraging participation)

Education as Preparation for Participation in Worship

Preparation for active participation in worship is an important part of the congregation's educational ministry with children, parents, and persons of all ages.

> In the exercise of its responsibility to encourage participation of its people in worship, the session should provide for education in Christian worship by means appropriate to the age, interests, and circumstances of the members of the congregation (Directory for Worship, W-1.4007).

Worship has its own vocabulary, practices, rhythms, and forms of expression. Teaching persons of all ages about these terms, practices, rhythms, and expressions is one of the most important ways to nurture effective participation in worship. Through age-appropriate educational experiences, children's readiness for and capacity to take part in the various parts of the worship service can be heightened. Including parents in these educational endeavors can greatly enrich them as matters of the faith are mutually explored and relationships are deepened. It is important to remember that increasing understanding of anything takes time for anyone. A child doesn't learn to walk or to play an instrument or a sport in a day. It takes practice, participation, patience, and repetition. The same is true of worshiping.

NOTES

1. William H. Willimon, *Preaching and Leading Worship* (Louisville, KY: Westminster John Knox Press, 1984), 23–24.

2. W. Alan Smith, *Children Belong in Worship: A Guide to the Children's Sermon* (St. Louis: CBP Press, 1984), 55.

3. Margie Morris, in *Helping Children Feel at Home in Church* (Nashville: Discipleship Resources, 1988), points out that "if every child who attends worship has a chance to get to know the pastor at other times, or if children are so naturally integrated into the service as leaders and participants that they intrinsically know their worth in the Christian community, we could dispense with a special time set aside for children" (p. 58).

4. Gobbel, A. Roger, and Phillip C. Huber. *Creative Designs with Children at Worship* (Atlanta: John Knox Press, 1981), 14.

5. Adapted from Carolyn Brown, *You Can Preach to the Kids, Too! Designing Sermons for Adults and Children* (Nashville: Abingdon Press, 1997), 45–56, and from David Ng, "Encouraging Children to Hear the Word of God," in *Reformed Liturgy and Music*, XXV, 1, Winter 1992, published by the Theology and Worship Ministry Unit of the Presbyterian Church (U.S.A.), 26–27.

6. See note 5.

RESOURCES

Children and Worship

The Constitution of the Presbyterian Church (U.S.A.), Part II, Book of Order (Louisville, KY: Office of the General Assembly, 2001).

Brown, Carolyn C. *Gateways to Worship: A Year of Worship Experiences for Young Children*. (Nashville: Abingdon, 1989).

_____. *Forbid Them Not: Involving Children in Sunday Worship*. (Based on the Common Lectionary, Year A). Nashville: Abingdon, 1992.

_____. *Forbid Them Not: Involving Children in Sunday Worship*. (Based on the Common Lectionary, Year B). Nashville: Abingdon, 1993.

_____. *Forbid Them Not: Involving Children in Sunday Worship*. (Based on the Common Lectionary, Year C). Nashville: Abingdon, 1994.

_____. *You Can Preach to the Kids, Too! Designing Sermons for Adults and Children* (Nashville: Abingdon Press, 1997).

Caldwell, Elizabeth Francis. *Come Unto Me, Rethinking the Sacraments for Children* (Cleveland: United Church Press, 1996).

Castleman, Robbie. *Parenting in the Pew: Guiding Your Children into the Joy of Worship* (Downers Grove, IL: InterVarsity Press, 2002).

Dawn, Marva J. *Is It a Lost Cause? Having the Heart of God for the Church's Children* (Grand Rapids: Eerdmans, 1997).

Duckert, Mary. *New Kid in the Pew: Shared Ministry with Children* (Louisville, KY: Westminster John Knox Press, 1991).

Henderson, Dorothy. *45 Ways to Involve Children in Worship* (Ontario: Presbyterian Church in Canada, 1997).

Juengst, Sara Covin. *Sharing Faith with Children: Rethinking the Children's Sermon* (Louisville, KY: Westminster John Knox Press, 1994).

Morris, Margie *Helping Children Feel at Home in Church*. Rev. ed. (Nashville: Discipleship Resources, 1997).

Sandell, Elizabeth J. *Including Children in Worship: A Planning Guide for Congregations* (Minneapolis: Augsburg, 1991).

Smith, W. Alan. *Children Belong in Worship: A Guide to the Children's Sermon* (St. Louis: CSP Press, 1984).

Witvliet, John D., ed. *A Child Shall Lead Them: Children in Worship* (Garland, TX: Choristers Guild, 1999).

Children's Books
Boling, Ruth, Lauren J. Muzzy, and Laurie A. Vance. *A Children's Guide to Worship* (Louisville, KY: Geneva Press, 1997).

Getty-Sullivan, Mary Ann. *God Speaks to Us in Water Stories* (Collegeville, MN: Liturgical Press, 1996).

_____. *God Speaks to Us in Feeding Stories* (Collegeville, MN: Liturgical Press, 1997).

Grimes, Nikki. *Come Sunday*. (Grand Rapids: Eerdmans, 1996).

Ramshaw, Gail. *Sunday Morning*. (Chicago: Liturgy Training Publications, 1993).

_____ *Everyday and Sunday, Too*. (Minneapolis: Augsburg Press, 1997).

_____ *1–2–3 Church*. (Minneapolis: Augsburg Press, 1997).

Worship Education Resources for Adults

Chapman, Dean W. *How to Worship as a Presbyterian*. (Louisville, KY: Geneva Press, 2001). Explores the implications of the doctrine of the priesthood of all believers and discusses the worshiper's role in prayer, music, the reading and exposition of Scripture, the offering, and the Lord's Supper. Discussion questions are provided.

Hough, Debbie and Mary Emery Speedy. *Children in the Sanctuary: Involving Children Fully in the Worship Life of a Congregation* (Published for the Presbyterian and Reformed Educational Partnership by Church Leader Support, Presbyterian Church (U.S.A.), Louisville, KY, 2002). Looks at the participation of children in worship—the opportunities and challenges. The study guide can be ordered with an accompanying video or DVD.

Kline, C. Benton. *A Study Guide for the Directory for Worship*.(Louisville, KY: Presbyterian Publishing House, 1990). Written to help acquaint congregations with the Directory for Worship and to guide them in its use in the life of the church.

Noren, Carol M. *What Happens Sunday Morning: A Layperson's Guide to Worship* (Louisville, KY: Westminster John Knox Press, 1992). Raises consciousness about what we do in worship and why we do it.

Models for Worship Education with Children and Their Families

Brown, Carolyn C. *Gateways to Worship, A Year of Worship Experiences for Young Children*. (Nashville: Abingdon Press, 1989). Provides 52 session plans for introducing kindergartners and first-graders to worship.

Lou, Sue, Jean Floyd Love, Mickey Myers, and Sylvia Washer. *Get Ready! Get Set! Worship!* (Louisville, KY: Westminster John Knox Press, 1999). Provides 4 study sessions for adults and a number of models for helping children and parents explore and deepen their understanding of worship, baptism, and communion. Learning center designs and games are included.

Norton, Mary Jane Pierce. *Children Worship!* (Nashville: Discipleship Resources, 1997). Provides 13 sessions focusing on the 6 actions of worship, reproducible bulletin inserts, sample letters to parents and suggestions for church-wide study on children and worship.

Stewart, Sonja M., and Jerome W. Berryman. *Young Children and Worship*. (Louisville, KY: Westminster John Knox Press, 1989). Provides a way to introduce children ages 3–7 to the meaning and actions of corporate worship in a sensorimotor way. Approach is based on the Montessori method.

Children and the Mission and Outreach Committee

Sara Covin Juengst

When I was a child, I eagerly looked forward to the annual visits of missionaries to our church during "Foreign Missions Season," which was the first three months of the year. Two kinds of missionaries came—"home missionaries" who served in the United States and "foreign missionaries" who served overseas. I remember the enthusiasm and energy of "Miss Patsy" Turner as she told about her mission work in "Bloody Breathitt" County in the mountains of Kentucky, where teachers routinely carried guns to school for protection against bears and bearish humans.

The foreign missionaries stirred my imagination most, however, with their fascinating tales of ministry in exotic places. They told us of their ministry with Chinese women whose bound feet doomed them to limited lives. They told us of how they shared the stories of Jesus with enraptured African children gathered in the shade of mango trees. They spoke of building churches and schools in Mexico, Brazil, Japan, and Korea. I was impressed, not only by the exotic places, but by something more intangible: I was impressed with the passion and devotion of those missionaries. I was impressed with the sacrifices they had made to take the gospel to every nation, although I was only dimly aware of what the gospel was and of where those nations were. I was impressed that they were telling the stories of Jesus because they loved both the stories and the people to whom they were telling them. Who knows how much influence these childhood experiences had on my decision to become a missionary? Of one thing I am confident—those early experiences stamped me with a lifelong passion for the Great Commission and an earnest desire to find ways in which I could obey its call. My own experience reveals that children are not only fascinated by the mission and outreach arm of the church's ministry, but are also capable of becoming part of it. The church needs to seriously consider how we can draw upon the natural fascination and innate benevolence of children to enable them to have a role in taking the gospel to every nation.

According to the *Book of Order* of the Presbyterian Church (U.S.A.), the first great end of the church is "the proclamation of the gospel for the salvation of humankind" (G-1.0200). This task is basic for the life of the church, but it may seem too heavy a concept for young children. Interviews with children have found that although the abstract idea of "mission" may be difficult for children to grasp, they are capable of understanding concrete terms associated with mission. Children can understand, for example, that a missionary is a person who is sent to tell others about Jesus; that a mission field is an area where missionaries work; that churches send money to help support missionaries. Some children can even identify Paul as a missionary.[1]

The challenge of the church, therefore, is to find a concrete vocabulary that makes the first *Great End of the Church* come alive for children. One hindrance, however, is that adults are also often confused about what the word "mission" means. To many, "mission" means sending and supporting others to "do mission" in distant places. Jesus' attributing the fulfillment of Isa. 61:1–2 to himself and his ministry, however, implies that Christian mission requires becoming *personally* involved with persons in physical and spiritual need.

> The scroll of the prophet Isaiah was given to him. He unrolled the scroll and found the place where it was written:
> "The spirit of the Lord is upon me,
> because he has anointed me
> to bring good news to the poor.
> He has sent me to proclaim
> release to the captives
>   and recovery of sight to the blind,
>   to let the oppressed go free,
> to proclaim the year of the Lord's favor."
> Then he began to say to them, "Today this scripture has been fulfilled in your hearing" (Luke 4:17–19, 21).

Mission is not done only within the walls of the church. It takes place wherever there is special need.[2] Children need to be encouraged to think of mission in this way. They need to see adults giving time as well as money to mission—locally and globally. They need to know that their churches take mission seriously. However, since children learn best by doing, they will learn about mission most effectively when they are involved in doing mission. It is important to keep this in mind as the mission and outreach committee goes about its work.

The Tasks of the Mission and Outreach Committee

The mission and outreach committee has three important tasks in the education of children: 1. to educate children about mission, 2. to educate children for mission, and 3. to educate children in mission.[3] Education *about* mission means learning about the mission work of the church and understanding how missionaries are called and supported and the kinds of work that they do. Being educated *for* mission means being inspired to make a commitment to support and service, being exposed to different places and people, becoming appreciative of Christianity as it is lived out in a variety of cultures, and developing acceptance of others. Being educated *in* mission means coming to understand through *participation* in outreach to our own families and our neighborhoods that "mission" refers not only to reaching out to distant lands and other cultures, but to sharing God's love at home.

This kind of mission education is most effective when it begins with children at an early age, so mission education really begins at home. Children are mixtures of narcissism and magnanimity. They are capable of extreme selfishness and extreme generosity. Mission education can help nurture healthy benevolence—care for others that is not self-deprecating—and lay the groundwork for genuine Christian commitment. When adults reach out to persons in need or work for justice, while not neglecting themselves or their families, they provide children a model of healthy benevolence. In families that practice healthy benevolence, children will learn to accept all persons, including themselves, as children of God and will come to see caring for others as a natural part of living. When families explore relationships with persons from other countries, children learn that Christian compassion does not stop at national borders. (Families that have taken part in such international exchange programs as Christmas International House, which was begun as a means for local churches to provide hospitality over the Christmas holidays for international students on nearby college campuses, have witnessed the powerful impact made on young children by developing friendships with international visitors.)[4] Part of the responsibility of the mission and outreach committee is to support families in their outreach efforts by providing guidance for balanced living and avenues for family involvement in mission.

Much of what the mission and outreach committee provides for children is incorporated in what it does for adults. Unfortunately, all too often the programs, studies, offerings, and even mission festivals are geared toward adults, with children kept on the sidelines. This may be due to two factors. First, since it is the adults who are the primary current supporters of the mission and outreach programs of the church through study, service projects, and giving, the contributions of children may be considered minor. The second factor is a practical one—the lack of knowledge of resources for mission and outreach education with children. Given the number of materials that flood church offices, it can be an overwhelming task to sort out relevant resources. Most of the brochures, catalogues, and advertisements about mission resources that reach the mission and outreach committee are aimed at adults.

The mission and outreach committee needs to make special efforts to enlist children in *concrete* mission-related activities, such as earning money for mission projects, collecting and sorting food for a local food pantry, helping in a soup kitchen or homeless shelter, making cards for shut-ins, and praying for and writing letters to missionaries. Past issues of the *Mission Yearbook for Prayer & Study* of the Presbyterian Church (U.S.A.)[5] are a great resource for bulletin board displays and creative mission projects such as mobiles, maps, and collages. Adding current news items from around the world to items from the *Mission Yearbook* will contextualize mission education, making it seem current and relevant. One church school teacher contributed this idea:

> On a child's birthday, the teacher reads the information for that day in the *Mission Yearbook*. One or two of the names of the persons listed for that day are written on a card, with the child's name placed at the top. The child attaches the card to the border of a world map located on a bulletin board or wall. The card is then connected by a string to the site of the mission work.

In all of these hands-on activities, children need to feel that their own efforts are taken seriously by the rest of the congregation. Attention can be called to their efforts through the church newsletter or bulletin, in bulletin board displays, and during worship services.

Getting Started

The outline for the work of the mission and outreach committee is guided by the following goals.

Children will:

- understand what the "Great Commission" means
- see specific ways their churches and denomination help others through outreach and stewardship
- discover ways to share the Christian faith at home and abroad
- become aware of the needs of others around the world
- develop concern and compassion for others

- interact with missionaries, national church leaders, and people from other cultures
- help plan and participate in mission projects

Schedule a Brainstorming and Planning Session

1. *Invite* the pastor, the director of Christian education, and one or more persons involved in the church's ministries with children to meet with the committee for this session.
2. *Gather* resources. Visit your middle governing body's resource center, or ask the resource center coordinator to send you resource books on mission education for children.
3. *Make* a large chart of special days in the church year that pertain to mission and outreach. A suggested calendar is provided below.

Convene the Brainstorming and Planning Session

1. *Open* with prayer and Scripture. You might use Matt. 28:19–20 and Luke 4:18–19, or any of the selections listed below under "Resources."
2. *Explore* the meaning of mission.
   The following exercise might be useful for identifying a working understanding of mission.

   Step 1: Distribute copies of *Assumptions*, found on page 171 of this resource, inviting the group members to imagine that they are members of a task force commissioned to determine the mission policy of your denomination for the next five years.

   Step 2: Ask individuals to review the list of assumptions, cross out those statements with which they do not agree and add to the list as they see fit, then rank remaining statements in order, with number one the most important.

   Step 3: Have the individuals compare their lists and seek a consensus on the six most important assumptions. This consensus will serve as a working definition of mission.
3. *Brainstorm* ideas
   Begin by listing everything your church is currently doing for mission and outreach. Next, put a check by each one of these items that involves children or has the potential to involve children. Then spend some time considering other possibilities, especially those for which children are *uniquely* qualified. This would be a good time to explore suggestions from resource books.
4. *Develop* a calendar for the year.

It is important that mission education not be limited to one season of the year or to one offering. Here are some ideas for tying the mission education of children to the church calendar, holidays, and special offerings.

- *January*

  Epiphany. In many church traditions, Epiphany is a time to commemorate the coming of the magi who brought gifts to the Christ child. Suggested activity: set up an Epiphany bank in the church and encourage children to show their thankfulness for the gifts they received at Christmas by making gifts to mission. For example, they could donate a nickel for each gift they received.

  Week of Prayer for Christian Unity. The Week of Prayer for Christian Unity is generally celebrated during the third week in January. Suggested activity: Have children make posters illustrating what it means for people to live together in unity and peace. Display these posters in a prominent place during the Week of Prayer for Christian Unity.

- *February*

  Black History Month. A Black History Kit that includes a teacher's manual and reproducible materials for children, youth, and adults is available from Presbyterian Distribution Service. Children can honor African Americans in the Presbyterian Church by writing essays or poems or by creating posters celebrating the accomplishments of African American Presbyterians. They can also celebrate current national or regional staff, local pastors and educators, and those serving on middle governing body committees by writing letters or offering special prayers.

  Mission Festival. Include children and youth in planning a mission festival for the whole congregation with songs, dances, and food from around the world. Use overseas area profiles in the *Mission Yearbook* as resource material. If a special missionary guest is invited, ask him or her to bring artifacts, pictures, and maps that would interest the children as well as the adults. Children could host this celebration, helping to plan the focus, activities, and menu and helping to make decorations, which might include flags of different nations and displays of pictures highlighting the church's mission work in featured areas.

- *March*

  Lent. Lent is a good time to focus on sacrificial ways to show our love of God by reaching out to the world around us. The emphasis is on *doing* love. Children can write notes of appreciation to their parents, pastors, teachers, and best friends. They also can make greeting cards for persons in the congregation who are ill or write a letters of encouragement to missionaries.

  World Day of Prayer. Help children write a prayer for Christians in other places. Ask them to name countries, especially where there is suffering caused by war, hunger, or natural disasters. List the places on newsprint and use them as responses to the petition, "O loving God, we pray for the people of . . ." Conclude with a prayer of thanksgiving for Christians in other nations. The children can present this prayer as a part of the congregational worship service on the Sunday before the World Day of Prayer.

- *April*

  One Great Hour of Sharing. In the Presbyterian Church (U.S.A.), the One Great Hour of Sharing offering is traditionally taken on Easter Sunday. Publicity packets are sent to churches from Mission Education and Promotion, Congregational Ministries Publishing, and contain excellent ideas for children.

- *May*

  Christian Family Week. One of the best ways for children to become interested in other countries and cultures is by getting to know individuals from those places. Encourage families with children in the congregation to host international guests. This could be as simple as inviting international students from nearby schools to dinner or welcoming international visitors to the United States into the home. The United States SERVAS Committee brings together host families and international visitors.[6]

  Access Sunday. Access Sunday is dedicated to raising issues related to disabilities. A free packet, which often includes materials for children, is available from PHEWA at 1-888-728-7228, ext. 8100.

Pentecost. Pentecost can be thought of as the day when the mission work of the church truly began. Children might plan a birthday party for the church, or help plan the Pentecost Offering. One group of children gave the gift of time and creativity when they assembled over fifty boxes with children's scissors, colored paper, stencils, crayons, pencils, and glue to be sent overseas to benefit school children in Ghana.[7]

- *June*

Vacation Church School. Plan a mission-centered emphasis for children, using one of the Friendship Press study books listed in the Resources beginning on p. 168.

- *July*

Clean World Day. In preparation for "Clean World Day," you may want to do a study such as *God's Good World: A Peacemaking Resource for Children* or *Tobee and the Amazing Bird Choir* by Chloe Canterbury, (Louisville: Bridge Resources, 1999). Both are available from Presbyterian Distribution Service. Many activities can help children come to see that care for creation is an essential part of Christian mission. Some suggestions are offered below. Other activities can be found on the Presbyterians for Restoring Creation Web site at www.pcusa.org/prc.

  - Set aside a day to clean up the area around the church, a local park, or a school yard. Children can work with adults picking up litter and collecting recyclable cans and bottles. Children can make trash bags for collecting litter by taking old paper bags or shopping bags, placing a plastic bag inside as a lining, and adding strong handles of cord. Bags can be decorated with pictures, phrases, and the church name. Any money received by recycling can be donated toward a mission project.
  - Plan a recycle day for the elderly or shut-in who may have difficulty recycling. With the help of adults, children can pick up recyclables and deliver them to a recycling center. Any money received can be donated toward a mission project.

- *August*
  Back to School. As children prepare to return to school, it is a good time for them to be reminded of those who are less fortunate. Work with a local outreach center to prepare back to school kits containing notebooks, paper, pens, pencils, and other items for children who will not be able to go shopping for school supplies. This is also an important time to remind children of their role in demonstrating the love of God at school. Sunday school and worship prior to the first day of school can be dedicated to lessons on accepting all people and God's special concern for the outcast. Offering a dedicatory prayer for children during the worship service will emphasize their importance as they set off to the school "mission field."

- *September*
  Evangelism Sunday. Arrange for children to serve as greeters at church, particularly to other children. Help the children create a welcome flyer to be given to visiting children to tell them about how their church cares for and about children.[8]
  Native American Day. Celebrate the Presbyterian Church (U.S.A.)'s ministries with and by Native American peoples. Children in Eurocentric churches could develop pen-pal relationships with children in Native American congregations to learn how different tribal groups express Christian faith in the context of their heritages. It is important to keep in mind that the term "Native Americans" refers to numerous distinct cultures, each with its own history and heritage. For more information on Native American Presbyterian ministries or for a celebration packet, contact the Racial Ethnic Ministries Office of the National Ministries Division of the PC(USA) at (888) 728-7228, ext. 5684. *Crickets and Corn: Five Stories About Native North Americans* from Friendship Press is an excellent resource for exploring Native American cultures with children.

- *October*
  World Food Day. Take the children on a field trip to a local food pantry or invite a worker from the pantry to speak to the group. Develop a list of good items to donate—the director

of the pantry can help. Discuss with the children creative ways of collecting and giving these items. In some churches, children place their items on the altar during the Communion service as a way of putting their gifts before God. In one church, the children created a labyrinth out of canned goods and invited church members to engage in the spiritual practice of walking the labyrinth before items were taken to the pantry.

World Communion Sunday. The first Sunday in October has traditionally been a time to celebrate World Communion Sunday and to receive the Peacemaking Offering. Encourage the children's choir to learn the chorus to "Jesus Loves Me," "Jesus Loves the Little Children," or "He's Got the Whole World in His Hands" in several different languages and sing it in these languages as part of the worship service.[9]

- *November*

  Stewardship Dedication Sunday. The Stu Bear resources packet, developed by Stewardship Education, Congregational Ministries Division, PC(USA), is available in English, Spanish, and Korean. An accompanying audiocassette of story and songs is also available. Call Presbyterian Distribution Service at (800) 524-2612.

- *December*

  Advent/Christmas. Encourage children to participate in the Christmas Joy offering. Fifty percent of this offering goes to support the eight Presbyterian-related racial ethnic schools and colleges, and the other half goes to the Board of Pensions assistance programs. Visit the Web site at http://www.pcusa.org/cjoffering/kid.htm for children's activities. Children can also help make the holidays brighter for less fortunate children by bringing in outgrown toys in good condition to be donated to local organizations. Older children can help serve Christmas dinner at a local outreach program.

5. Identify needed materials and resources.
6. Plan for global awareness education for teachers and children. Each year, Friendship Press, an arm of the National Council of Churches, publishes excellent educational materials on mission

for children and adults. Global awareness education for teachers is better done prior to that of children. Summer vacation Bible/church school would be a good time for global awareness education for children.

7. Delegate responsibilities. The best laid plans can collapse if responsibility is not properly designated and carried out.

Assumptions[10]

Directions: Draw a line through the statements below with which you do not agree. Add any assumptions to the list that you think are missing. Rank in order the remaining statements with number one the most important.

Compare your lists with the rest of the group and come to a consensus on the six most important assumptions.

Mission means:

Bringing the gospel to unreached people

Sending missionaries to other countries

Preaching liberation to oppressed people

Converting people to a Western way of life

Being culturally sensitive

Helping people raise their living standard

Giving money to support missionaries

Providing hospitals, schools, and day-care facilities

Witnessing to God's love wherever we are

Working for peace and justice

Helping people who help themselves

Working with partner churches

Listening to people

Recognizing our interdependency with others

Loving our neighbors

Demonstrating responsibility for the welfare of our planet

Reaching out to people in the communities in which we live

Other

Permission is granted to make photocopies of this page.

NOTES

1. D-B Heusser and Phyllis Heusser, *Children as Partners in the Church* (Valley Forge, PA: Judson Press, 1985), 53.

2. Ibid., 54.

3. Faye Wilson-Beach, *Great Mission Ideas for Workers with Children* (Cincinnati: General Board of Global Ministries, United Methodist Church, 1990), 1.

4. Churches provide lodging, meals, entertainment, sightseeing, and worship for their guests. For brochures or further information on the Christmas International House, call Susan Craig at (404) 228-7749.

5. The *Mission Yearbook for Prayer & Study* is available from Mission Education and Promotion, a ministry of the General Assembly Council of the Presbyterian Church (U.S.A.), (800) 524-2612. The leaflet *Take Time to Pray and Study* (PDS 70-612-02-425) provides many ideas for using the *Mission Yearbook* in mission education.

6. Write to United States SERVAS Committee, Inc., 11 John Street, Room 406, New York, NY, 10038, or call (212) 267-0252.

7. Gretchen Micka, "Kids as Caretakers: Overcoming Steward Shock," in *Faithfulness Sustains the Generations*, v.1, Part Two (Louisville: Office of Stewardship, Congregational Ministries Division, PC(USA), 1999), 18.

8. Faye Wilson-Beach, 38.

9. Sara C. Juengst, ed., *Messengers of God's Love: Involving Children in Mission* (Louisville, KY: PC(USA), 1992), III-43.

10. Adapted from Arthur O. F. Bauer, *Making Mission Happen* (New York: Friendship Press, 1977), 18.

RESOURCES

Scripture

The most important resource is the Bible itself. The risen Christ commissioned his followers to witness to God's love for the world through word and deed. This commission cannot be understood apart from the story of God's action in the world, which we find in the Scriptures of the Old and New Testaments. Below are some key biblical passages.

- Mission as good news: Matthew 28:16–20 (The Great Commission); Luke 4:16–21 (Jesus' sermon in the synagogue at Capernaum)
- Mission as sharing the good news: Acts 8:26–40 (Philip and the Ethiopian); Acts 16:9–10 (Paul's call to Macedonia)
- Mission as justice: Isaiah 42:1–4 (God's servant and justice); Micah: 6:6–8 (What God wants from us)
- Mission as right living: Acts: 2:44–48; I Thess. 1:4–8

Mission Study Books for Children from Friendship Press

Friendship Press, an ecumenical publisher of educational materials for schools and congregations in the United States and Canada, has a selection of over 200 books and resources, many of them with companion study guides to help educators and study leaders plan their curricula. The Presbyterian Church (U.S.A.) is one of eighteen denominational partners in the development and publication of these mission study resources. Included in these resources are study books for children on mission in geographical areas such as the Philippines, Japan, the Caribbean, Africa, and Bangladesh. All have teachers' guides. There are also study books for children that address understanding people from other cultures and traditions; the issue of poverty; educating children for social responsibility; children with disabilities; children at risk; and native North American children. These usually contain six sessions and can be used as special studies for children in the summer (as part of vacation Bible schools, for example), on Sunday evenings, or in conjunction with church suppers.

Friendship Press also provides some excellent resource books for creative activities to promote global awareness: *Make a World of Difference*, *Creative Activities for Global Learning*, and *The Children's World Series*, which includes three volumes of stories, songs, and games from every continent. A 24-page magazine, *All Quite Beautiful*, invites children to learn about people from cultures and traditions different from their own through Bible readings, stories, and activities. Friendship Press books may be ordered by calling (800) 889-5733, or by writing Friendship Press, 475 Riverside Drive, Room 860, New York, NY 10115. (*All Quite Beautiful* is also available from Presbyterian Distribution Service.)

Mission Yearbook for Prayer & Study

The *Mission Yearbook for Prayer & Study*, published by Mission Education and Promotion, Congregational Ministries Publishing, a ministry of the General Assembly Council of the Presbyterian Church (U.S.A.), is an indispensable tool for a mission and outreach committee. This publication gives a picture of the ministry of Presbyterians throughout the world. For each day of the year, it offers a choice of Scripture selections to read and several paragraphs describing a particular mission project. A free leaflet, *Take Time to Pray and Study*, contains many ideas for effective use of the *Mission Yearbook* for mission education and promotion. The *Mission Yearbook for Prayer & Study* and *Take Time to Pray and Study* can be ordered by calling (800) 524-2612. Check out the *Mission Yearbook* Web site at www.pcusa.org/pcusa/cmd/mip/mybtoday.html

Children's Mission Yearbook for Prayer & Study

Children's Mission Yearbook for Prayer & Study debuted in 2003. Adapted from the widely used *Mission Yearbook for Prayer & Study*, the new resource is a personal devotional guide for third through fifth graders. It includes prayers, PC(USA) mission stories from around he world, maps, photos, puzzles and games. It can be appropriately used for family devotions, church school classes, and children's worship. Order from Presbyterian Distribution Service at (800) 524-2612. PDS 70-612-03-451.

Mission Resources Available from Presbyterian Distribution Service; call (800) 524-2612 or visit www.pds.pcusa.org

Africa: Bad News to Good News Kid's Pages

This three-lesson kit enables children to learn about the causes of hunger, particularly in Africa, to take action on behalf of hungry children, and to understand that there is hope for Africa.

All Quite Beautiful

This 24-page magazine produced by Friendship Press invites children to learn about people from cultures and traditions different from their own through Bible readings, stories, and activities. An accompanying teacher's guide also is available.

Black History Kit

Kit includes a teacher's manual and reproducible materials for children, youth, and adults. Item number is 094075.

God's Good World: A Peacemaking Resource for Children

Designed for third- through sixth-grade children, this five-session resource was created to "assist older elementary students in discovering that they are called to love and care for the world that God made." It is ideal for a vacation Bible school. The item number is 70-270-97-002.

Mission Activity Place Mats

These place mats feature intergenerational activities designed to increase awareness of PC(USA) mission. One side, appropriate for young children, offers a hunt-and-find drawing in cartoon style of people doing good deeds. The other side features a brief mission story and has a multiple-choice quiz about mission. They are sold in a pack of 50.

Tobee and the Amazing Bird Choir

By Chloe Canterbury (Louisville: Bridge Resources, 1999). This book for older children explores many themes including the value of God's creation, the nature of human relationships with animals, happiness, courage, liberation, heroism, the risks of judging others, the significance of family, the process of maturation, and the importance of self-knowledge. Discussion questions are provided at the end of each chapter. The item number is 095603.

Walking with Africans: Continuing the Journey

This is an anthology of African blessings, stories, hymns, recipes, and other items. The item number is 70-350-95-650.

The Building Blocks of Stewardship
Elaine Barnett

Helping children understand the connections between giving, serving, and faith is a wonderful opportunity, as well as a critical responsibility shared by parents, church school teachers, members of the stewardship committee, and other adults within the church. Helping children make these connections in ways that have a lifelong impact involves more than coming up with gimmicks or gathering activities, more than receiving a perfunctory offering, and more than an occasional conversation about giving. There are a number of building blocks that must be in place for leaders as they endeavor to help children grow as stewards. These include adopting an understanding of stewardship as managing God's gifts, feeling comfortable talking about money, creating a climate of generosity, providing opportunities to practice generosity, and focusing on appropriate motivations for giving.

Building Block Number One: Adopting an Understanding of Stewardship as Managing God's Gifts

For adults to guide children, they must first have a solid theological understanding of stewardship. Faithful Christian stewardship begins with the recognition that stewardship is about how we take care of something that belongs to God and has been entrusted to us. The word "steward" comes from *stiweard* in the Old English from *stig*, meaning "house," and *weard* meaning "ward," so the steward is the ward of the house.[1] Our Hebrew ancestors understood their role as the guardians of the creation, as Genesis 2:15 indicates: "The Lord God took the man and put him in the Garden of Eden to till it and keep it."[2] First Corinthians 4:12 speaks of Christians having been given a trust in which they must prove themselves faithful.

Often stewardship is thought of as having to do with giving when it actually has more to do with caring for or managing.

> The term *stewardship* today is often used loosely to mean nothing more than "giving" or "'teaching about giving." But it always carries a spiritual or theological meaning that distinguishes it from institutional fund-raising. Stewardship involves more than money and more than expecting to be blessed in return. It includes the use of time, talent, and treasure and also the entire human family and the environment.[3]

A faithful steward manages all aspects of the gifts that God gives to an individual or a community. A good steward holds these gifts in trust before using them wisely for the good of all. Adults need to see themselves as stewards,[4] responsible for taking care of all the resources given them by God, as a first step in helping children reach that same understanding. They can then move toward teaching children that no matter their age, God has entrusted each of them with resources that can be used to fulfill God's mission.

Here are some suggestions for activities with children:

- *Rephrasing a common question.* "What do *you* want to *be* when you grow up?" This commonly asked question reflects prevailing cultural values, such as people *are* what they *do*, people should do what satisfies them, money means success, and being successful is an end that justifies all means. Rephrasing the question as "What do you think *God* wants you to *do* when you grow up?" emphasizes the fact that vocation is what a person does, not the sum total of a person's identity. This version of the question also raises up the belief that our lives belong to God and our vocational choices are acts of stewardship.

- *The Gift Tree.* Provide each child with an outline of a tree that shows its roots and branches. (A photocopiable sample is provided on page 184 of this resource.) Ask the children to consider the gifts that God has given them. You may need to encourage children to think beyond traditional gifts such as musical ability and athleticism. Encourage them to think about what they enjoy doing, about how people describe them, (e.g., "She's a talker," can be reframed as being friendly and outgoing; "He's a loner," may suggest a deep thinker), and what dreams they have. Have the children write their gifts on the roots of the tree. Then have the children write in the branches the ways their gifts are or could be used in their lives. Encourage them to keep some of the roots and branches empty to indicate the wonderful things they will discover about themselves and life over the years. Children who are comfortable doing so can share their trees with one another. The trees can be displayed in a church school room, fellowship hall, or even sanctuary as a reminder of the importance of celebrating everyone's gifts. A prayer of thanksgiving and dedication may be offered once the trees are completed.

- *Stu Bear Storybook*. *Stu Bear—A Story about Stewardship for Young Children* is a good way to introduce children to a broad definition of stewardship that includes giving food to the needy, visiting the elderly, taking care of creation, taking care of oneself, and giving money. The *Stu Bear Storybook* is produced by Stewardship Education, Congregational Ministries Division, Presbyterian Church, (U.S.A.).

Building Block Number Two: Feeling Comfortable Talking About Money

In my experience, Presbyterians have a difficult time talking about stewardship, particularly financial stewardship, because of the very personal nature of the subject: consequently, money rarely is directly mentioned. For much of our history as a denomination, it seems we didn't need to remind people of their responsibilities to God because people understood giving as they understood all of their lives as belonging to God.[5] Today we must find ways to talk about giving and serving in financial matters.

Jesus spoke often of the use of money and the relationship of money to one's life. Twenty of the thirty-nine parables he taught have to do with stewardship and giving. According to *The Big Book of Presbyterian Stewardship*, if pastors preached the same percentage of sermons on stewardship as Jesus told parables on money and stewardship, congregations would hear seventeen sermons on stewardship each year.[6] From my experience as an educator, church member, and stewardship consultant, I've concluded that many congregations hear one or maybe two sermons on stewardship each year, and often the emphasis is on raising a budget rather than on living out gratitude to God.[7] Pastors are among those who need to become comfortable talking about money, both for their own spiritual maturity and so they can help others feel comfortable.

I suspect that the emphasis on unified giving to a budget has inhibited the growth of good stewardship in many congregations. When stewardship is addressed only once a year and only in terms of financial stewardship geared toward raising the budget, opportunities are limited for persons to respond with generous hearts. Giving once to the annual stewardship campaign denies people the opportunity to respond throughout the year to special offerings, one-time appeals for projects, and emergencies in the local and extended community. Although there is a clear philosophy behind unified giving, perhaps this approach developed in part from the difficulty church leaders have in talking about money.

Part of the task of the stewardship committee is to help the adults in the congregation become comfortable talking about money so they can model healthy attitudes for children. A way of moving toward this comfort level is to encourage people to think about their money-related experiences growing up and how those experiences influence present attitudes toward money. The more adults get in touch with their feelings about money, the better able they will be to guide children in giving.

When I was about ten, the church where my family belonged launched a sizable building campaign for a new sanctuary. The church leaders visited all members of the congregation and indicated the amount of money the committee had determined each family should give to the campaign. The amount designated for our family was more than my parents thought we could really afford, so we had a family meeting to discuss this. First we did a study of Old and New Testament passages that deal with money, talents, giving, and sharing. We then talked about the gifts God had given us. Finally, we discussed ways we could honor the request from the church. After much discussion we decided that for the next three years, once a week we would have a supper of black-eyed peas and corn bread and give to the church the amount of money we saved with this budget meal. Now I doubt this one meal a week really raised all the money needed to honor the pledge, but, this time together helped us to learn to talk openly about money, made us understand that all we had came from God, and gave us a great sense of giving back what God had given us.

When I think of stewardship education and children, I think of a story about a little boy and his dad. While the two were on their way to church, the dad gave the little boy a nickel and a quarter, saying, "Son, you put whichever one of these you want into offering plate." During the offering the boy carefully placed the nickel in the plate. On the way home, the disappointed Dad said, "I noticed that you put the nickel in the plate. Why?" Whereupon the boy replied, "I read in the Bible that the Lord loves a cheerful giver, and I knew I would be more cheerful if I gave the nickel instead of the quarter." Perhaps the father would have been wise to offer a fuller explanation of stewardship when he gave the boy the coins.

Here are two suggestions for activities with children:

- *Stu Bear Offering Bank.* The Stu Bear bank, one of the resources developed by Stewardship Education, Congregational Ministries Division, PC(USA), provides an opportunity for children to talk about money and to develop a regular approach to giving. The bank is divided into three sections so young stewards can deposit their financial resources in areas of giving, saving, and spending. It is very effective to give a child ten pennies and have them first put a penny in the giving side, then put a penny in the saving side, and put the remaining eight pennies in the spending side.
- *Prioritizing requests.* Save the requests for money that you receive in the mail from nonprofit organizations that you might want to support. Decide quarterly on a total amount of money to give, and sit down with your children to discuss how to divide that amount. Talk about the mission of each organization, how the money you give will be used, and whether the organization's mission is in keeping with your family's values.

Building Block Number Three: Creating a Climate of Generosity

The Search Institute in Minneapolis, Minnesota, suggests that a crucial role for congregations is to nurture habits of giving and serving for the common good. Their research shows that for children and youth to grow up healthy and balanced, congregations must take seriously their responsibility to nurture habits of giving and serving—even among the very youngest participants. A key factor in nurturing habits of giving and serving is the creation of a climate or culture of generosity,[8] where repeated actions become lifetime habits. A congregation with a climate of generosity is characterized by commitment to the well-being of others, high esteem for children and youth, an ability to see connections between giving and faith, and an expectation of generosity on everyone's part. Within a culture of generosity, there is a willingness among members to do one's part in working for the common good and for addressing the needs of the world. Helping children learn to think of the needs of others can begin very young through sharing space and toys. Children can then be made aware, in an age-appropriate way, of social issues like hunger and homelessness. This is best accomplished through concrete activities such as bringing food to a food bank or sharing toys with children of a family whose home has been lost.

A congregation with a culture of generosity connects giving and serving to faith and to congregational traditions. These connections help children see that faith and giving are not just "Sunday" things, but permeate and shape everyday life. It is important for children to see the relationship between what is said and what is done. Lessons on stewardship are most meaningful when they are part of the ongoing religious education of children rather than when one or two isolated lessons on "giving" are offered in the church year. Congregations and families need to be safe places where children are cherished. Children need to be encouraged to give and serve in ways that correspond to their individual gifts. They need to be included as part of the total life of the congregation and recognized for their accomplishments. Participation in church programs, serving as acolytes, reading Scripture, receiving the offering, or presenting a special offering are ways in which children's presence in the congregation can be honored.

A climate of generosity presupposes that everyone in the congregation will participate in giving—not just adults or just church members, but people of all ages and friends of the congregation. This requires that efforts be made to let giving and serving permeate all aspects of the life of the congregation. The stewardship committee needs to work with the children's ministry or the education committee, or the entire church governing board to review the atmosphere of the congregation to determine where children are welcomed, present, and included and suggest additional ways to include children regularly in the life of the church. Offering a study of *An Asset Builder's Guide to Youth and Money* (see resource section) would provide concrete suggestions for adults in relating to children and youth. When planning the stewardship emphasis, the stewardship committee needs to be sure to include the witness of children, as well as that of adults, about the importance of the church in their lives. It isn't just coincidental when a congregation made up of people of all ages is also a congregation of people who are generous sharers of their time, talent, and treasure. There is a carefully planned strategy, an all-encompassing theology present, so that people participate joyfully in actions that lead to habits—habits of giving and serving for the common good.

Building Block Number Four: Providing Opportunities to Practice Generosity

As with any skill, generosity needs to be practiced. Through concrete expressions of generosity children can gain a sense of responsibility as persons of faith. For greatest impact, these opportunities must be well-planned, carefully executed, and reflected upon, and the results must be celebrated.

Children learn much about giving in the context of their families, so providing intergenerational study and service opportunities is a good way to live out the partnership between the stewardship committee and families. Completing the *Gift Tree* exercise in an intergenerational group will help children see that learning to be good stewards is a lifelong process.

Here are some suggestions for activities with children:

- Develop a minute for mission targeted at children for use in the church school or midweek program. It is always important to mention something children can do, individually or as a group, to help out, such as collecting toys for a family whose home burned or baking cookies for workers at a Habitat for Humanity building site.
- Identify opportunities for service around the church or let the group select a project such as planting flowers.
- Dedicate a lesson or two to self-care as stewardship. You might want to invite a health profession to come and talk about healthy eating, exercise, or even dealing with emotions.
- Dedicate a lesson or two to the care of creation as stewardship. Plan a field trip to a local recycling center or animal preserve.

Building Block Number Five: Focusing on Appropriate Motivation for Giving

People give and serve for a variety of reasons, which include guilt or fear of what will happen if a person doesn't give, a sense of duty, expectation of reciprocity from God, self-promotion, compassion, faith, and gratitude. However tempting, relying on guilt, duty, reciprocity, and self-promotion as motivations for giving has limited appeal and is theologically unsound.

> Stewardship is different from fund-raising. It puts its focus on the individual's need to give, not on the church's need to receive. It stresses giving as an aspect of spiritual life and of people's relationship with or to God, not as merely a matter of meeting an institutional budget. . . . A stronger appreciation of stewardship depends on seeing it in terms of one's relationship with God and on feeling gratitude for one's blessings.[9]

The Christian faith calls each person to give generously out of compassion, gratitude, and love. When conversation and activities about giving and serving motivate people of all ages through compassion, gratitude, and love, there is a greater chance of developing lifestyles of unselfish stewardship. The words "grace," "gratitude", and "gladness" come from the same family of words in Greek. It is important to help children experience the gladness of being given a gift that was totally undeserved and unearned and then help them make connections between that feeling of gladness and giving. A review of ways in which giving and serving are discussed in congregational life is essential—looking as much as possible through the eyes of children. Check out publicity and minutes for mission to see that they are designed to appeal to people's sense of compassion, gratitude, and love rather than fear, guilt, and self-glorification. As activities are planned, be sure that children can see how their giving and serving actually benefit others. The classic religious education book *Kathy Ann Kindergartner* records a child's natural responses to many things in church life. One story that highlights how children see things differently from adults involves Kathy Ann's response to giving during her Sunday school class.

> Mrs. Turner said, "Who can tell us what we do with our pennies?" . . . Mrs. Turner told us—we give our pennies to Jesus. . . . I saw a man come get our money. It wasn't Jesus. It was Joyce's daddy.[10]

This cute story stresses the importance of carefully planning words, activities, and personal witness so that children get the right impression.

I once heard a presenter tell the story of a time in history when, if a ruler of a country was converted to Christianity, his servants and soldiers also were required to be baptized. According to legend, the soldiers were the most reluctant to make a total commitment to this new faith and as they entered the baptismal waters kept their sword arms out of the water so their fighting would not be affected. I found parallels to contemporary Christians in this story, but it isn't the sword arm that is being kept out of the water. Rather, modern-day Christians often effectively keep their wallets outside the waters of baptism. Nonetheless, by our baptisms we are called to totally give ourselves and our lives to God.

The attitudes that are formed in children toward giving and serving will last a lifetime. The task of the stewardship committee is to help church members understand stewardship as the management of all of the gifts of God; become comfortable with talking about money; create a climate of generosity; practice giving and serving; and focus on compassion, gratitude, and love as motivations for giving.

The Gift Tree

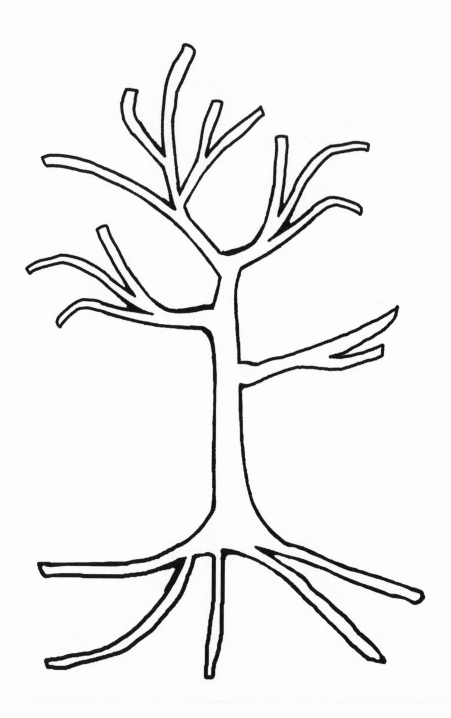

NOTES

1. *Webster's Ninth Collegiate Dictionary* (Springfield, MA: Merriam-Webster, Inc., 1991), 1157.

2. See also Genesis 1:28 and Psalm 8.

3. Dean R. Hoge, Charles E. Zech, Patrick H. McNamara, and Michael J. Donahue, *Money Matters: Personal Giving in American Churches* (Louisville, KY: Westminster John Knox Press, 1996), 144.

4. Peter Steinke, "Healthy Congregations Develop Generous People," Workshop 5, *Healthy Congregations Series* (Minneapolis: Lutheran Brotherhood, 2001), 18.

5. I base this conclusion on John Calvin's idea of "worshipful work," which implies that all that we do is an offering to God; on a review of early hymnals in which there are not obvious stewardship hymns; and on the fact that bazaars and other fund-raisers are fairly recent phenomena.

6. Elaine W. Barnett, Laura S. Gordon, and Margaret Hendrix, *The Big Book of Presbyterian Stewardship* (Louisville, KY: Geneva Press, 2000), ix.

7. I have had people apologize to me, when I have visited their church, for my having to be in their congregation for "that money sermon."

8. Eugene C. Roehlkepartain, *Kids Have A Lot to Give: How Congregations Can Nurture Habits of Giving and Serving for the Common Good* (Minneapolis: Search Institute, 1999), 18.

9. Dean R. Hoge, Charles E. Zech, Patrick H. McNamara, and Michael J. Donahue, *Money Matters: Personal Giving in American Churches* (Louisville, KY: Westminster John Knox Press, 1996), 144.

10. Frances Dunlap Heron, *Kathy Ann Kindergartner* (New York: Abingdon Press, 1955), 15–16.

RESOURCES

Books

The Big Book of Presbyterian Stewardship by Elaine W. Barnett, Laura S. Gordon, Margaret A. Hendrix, Louisville, KY: Geneva Press, 2000

An Asset Builder's Guide to Youth and Money by Jolene L. Roehlkepartain, Minneapolis: Search Institute, 1999

Growing Up Generous: Engaging Youth in Giving and Serving by Eugene Roehlkepartain, Elanah Dalyah Naftali, and Laura Musegades, Bethesda, MD: Alban Institute, 2000

Kid's Have a Lot to Give: How Congregations Can Nurture Habits of Giving and Serving by Eugene C. Roehlkepartain, Minneapolis: Search Institute, 1999

Educational Materials Available from Presbyterian Distribution Service

At One with Creation: An intergenerational video and study guide that portrays the beginning of the world as a reflection of God's love. Running time: 12 minutes. Produced by Stewardship Education, Congregational Ministries Division, Presbyterian Church (U.S.A.). Item number 227-93-200.

Ever Expanding Circles: An award-winning video curriculum for ages 10–14 in which seven youth explore the varied dimensions of stewardship. Produced by Stewardship Education, Congregational Ministries Division, Presbyterian Church (U.S.A.). Item number 70-370-97-502.

Special Places—Taking Care of God's World: A video for children ages 8–10 with stories of the sacred relationship between humans and creation that is told by three Native Americans against a backdrop of beautiful views of nature. Produced by Stewardship Education, Congregational Ministries Division, Presbyterian Church (U.S.A.). Item number 918-88-655.

The Stu Bear Packet, produced by Stewardship Education, Congregational Ministries Division, Presbyterian Church (U.S.A.), is designed to help children ages 3–6 begin to explore the meaning of responsible Christian discipleship in matters of time, talent, and money. Items in the program include the Stu Bear storybook, a coloring poster with stickers, an audiocassette with the story and songs, and an offering bank. Item number 70-370-95-209 (English); 70-370-95-217 (Korean); 70-370-95-216 (Spanish).

Stu Bear Goes on a Mission Visit. Storybook includes lesson plans. PDS 70-370-01-208.

Organizations

Office of Stewardship Education, Congregational Ministries Division, Presbyterian Church (U.S.A.)
100 Witherspoon Street
Louisville, KY 40202
(888) 728-7228, ext. 5197
Web site: http://se.pcusa.org

Search Institute
615 First Avenue, NE, Suite 125
Minneapolis, MN 55413
(800) 888-7828
Web site: www.search-institute.org

The Property and Maintenance Committee Provides for Children

Carolyn Brown

It has been said that we shape our buildings and then they shape us. This is never truer than with the spaces we create and maintain for the children of the church. When we design our communal space with the presence of both children and adults in mind, we invite children to become part of the family of God's people. When we design children's nurseries and classrooms particularly for children and then maintain them with the same attention we lavish on the sanctuary, children grow up in them knowing that they are valued and respected. On the other hand, if we consistently insist that children accept uncomfortable adult-sized pews, tables, and chairs or send them off to unattractive and uncomfortable rooms, it will be almost impossible for them to believe that they are valued by the church, and, in turn, it will interfere with their sense of being loved and cherished children of God. The work of the property and maintenance committee on behalf of children is, therefore, critical to children's spiritual formation. In addition, the majority of young families who come to a given church for the first time do so because of and through their children. They enter a church building looking first for the children's space. Only after their children are settled will they move on to the adult space. Today's young parents are experienced evaluators of children's space. Their standards are high, and they will not leave their children in places that are dirty, crowded, or poorly equipped. This makes the work of the property and maintenance committee on behalf of children key to the church's outreach to young families and for church growth.

To begin its work on behalf of the children, the committee needs basic information on providing quality space for children. Fortunately, much work has been done in this field and there has been longstanding agreement about it. In the following pages, we will consider some basic criteria for children's spaces, age-specific needs, and how to deal with less-than-ideal conditions.

Some Basic Criteria

There are basic requirements for all children's spaces. These include space, safety, security, storage, equipment, and cleanliness.

Space. It is important to keep in mind that children have active, growing bodies. While adults are often comfortable seated around a table, extra space is essential for educational activities that are geared for children. Children need room to move, play, dance, and work on projects. When cramped for space, teachers tend to resort to less creative, less interesting learning activities, which bore children and can lead to discipline problems.

Safety. All children's rooms must be equipped for all emergencies. First aid kits and fire extinguishers must be kept up to date and stored in easily accessible places. There should be a plan for what groups will do to get out of the building or to the safest part of the building depending on the emergency. The plan for each room needs to be posted in every room and rehearsed occasionally. All groups need access to a phone for emergencies.

Security. We must protect children from dangerous people. Many churches now require young children to be signed in and out. Most use simple pencil and paper systems. Many also give parents an identification card as they leave their children and require its return before they can pick them up. Shelves or narrow tables by doorways simplify this process. Infants and toddlers often are accepted and returned over Dutch doors or counters set across the doorway. Sign-in systems generally suffice on Sundays, but congregations that sponsor weekday kindergartens or day-care programs for young children need to look seriously at installing a limited-access security system to protect children from strangers or estranged family members. Such systems are seldom used on Sunday mornings.

Storage. Storage is absolutely critical in multiuse areas. Each group that uses a room needs storage *in that room*. Groups that use a building frequently need hallway storage for seasonal and bulkier items. This is especially important when weekday children's programs and children's church school classes share rooms. Clear, shared understandings about what can and cannot be shared among groups using the same space are essential. All stored materials need to be clearly labeled according to content, group, and whether or not it is *to be shared*.

Equipment. Child-sized tables and chairs are essential. Tables with adjustable legs are worth the investment. All children's classes need table tops of similar size. With them a table can be used for a variety of age groups. All equipment and toys need to be clean and safe, but not necessarily new. Many families are delighted to donate slightly used items they have outgrown. It is wise, however, to have an established a policy that the church accepts all donations and promises to pass on to others items that cannot be used. This policy needs to be repeated upon the acceptance of each donation. The church can then evaluate the sturdiness, appropriateness, and usefulness of gifts, keep what is needed, and deliver the rest to other organizations.

Cleanliness. Cleanliness is indispensable. Whether the space is ideal or "the best we can do at this point," the property and maintenance committee can make an enormous contribution by being sure the children's spaces are clean. Cleanliness in preschool areas, especially in nurseries where children put everything they touch into their mouths, should be hospital quality.

- Floors should be swept after each group's use and mopped at least monthly.
- Infant and toddler toys need to be washed in a one part (bleach) to ten parts (water) solution—monthly if used only on Sunday mornings or after each use when there is more frequent use.
- Children's bathrooms should be cleaned after each group's meeting.
- Dusting and other cleaning should be on the same schedule as the adult rooms and sanctuary.

This cleaning may be done, whether by paid staff or by church volunteers.

In addition to shared basic requirements, children's spaces have age-specific needs.

Permission is granted to make photocopies of this page.

Age-Specific Needs

Children's Spaces: Facts and Figures	Nursery (birth–age 2)	Preschool (2–5)	Elementary (grades 1–6)
Maximum Number of Children Per Room	8 children	15–18 children	16–25 children
Space Per Child (add 10% for storage)	30–35 square feet	30–35 square feet	25–30 square feet
Plumbing Requirements	sink for diapering	child-sized bathroom fixtures in off-room bathroom in-room sink for snack and project clean-up	hallway bathrooms and water fountains
Furnishings	sturdy rockers for adults cribs, washable rug, rocking chairs, changing table counter or hooks for diaper bags	30 inch x 36 inch x 18–20 inch tables; 8–10 inch chairs (10-inch difference between tables and chairs); hangers or hooks for coats	30 inch x 40–60 inch x 28–30 inch tables; 14–16 inch chairs (10-inch difference between tables and chairs); bulletin boards or cork strips; hangers or hooks for coats
Storage	closed cabinet for linens and diapering supplies	open shelves for toys in-room storage for art supplies and materials	open shelves for books in-room cabinets for art supplies, small audiovisual equipment, and curriculum resources

The Infant Nursery

The success of an infant nursery begins with its location. Parents arrive with car seats, diaper bags, and often older siblings in tow. Therefore, the nursery should be conveniently located. Nurseries on the ground floor save parents from toting loads up and down stairs and avoid delays by toddlers intent on climbing the stairs "all by myself." Though we generally expect nurseries to be located with or near older preschool classes, there is great value in thinking of them as adjunct to adult worship, education, and meeting spaces and locating them near those spaces.

Infants are best cared for in groups of no more than eight children with a minimum of two adults. Infants need a quiet, pleasant, scrupulously clean space decorated in soft colors. Washable floors topped by one or two cleanable, soft-colored area rugs make a good foundation. Walls decorated with simple, large figures like birds, flowers, the sun, and other familiar natural shapes attract the attention of both babies and adults. An in-room (preferably double) sink is essential for diaper changing and to bottle preparation. Daylight from large windows can create an airy, homey feeling.

The room needs to be furnished with sturdy cribs, rockers, changing tables, and supply closets. It is not necessary to provide a crib for every child because many will arrive in their car seats and will be happy to remain close to the action on the floor in the carrier. Do, however, stock enough crib sheets for every child so that sheets can be changed between children. If there routinely are more infants and toddlers than the caregivers could carry in their arms at once, be sure that one crib is an "evacuation crib," designed with special support and larger wheels to move up to eight infants at once in an emergency. A rocking chair large enough for an adult to feed and cuddle a child is needed for each adult attendant.

The Preschool Room

Preschoolers are active learners. They need clean, airy rooms furnished with child-sized tables and chairs and low shelves filled with attractively arranged toys. Large windows that are low enough for children to look through but not so low that they can run into or fall through them provide both light and the opportunity to ponder God's world as the seasons change.

Preschool children are best served by off-room bathrooms with child-sized plumbing. One bathroom located between two preschool rooms is particularly workable for younger children. Four- and five-year-olds enjoy using a hall bathroom if it is within sight and hearing of their room. In-room sinks ease cleanup after snacks and the messy projects preschoolers love and learn from.

When preschool rooms are shared by Sunday and weekday programs, there are special requirements. It is important to check state laws about the space in which groups of children may be cared for or taught. These regulations generally apply to preschool and day-care spaces, but not to Sunday and other congregational settings in which children are gathered for short periods of time. They can, however, provide guidance for all child-care endeavors. Among the Web sites with valuable information are those of the Department of Health and Human Services (www.hhs.gov), the Public Health Service (www.hhs.gov/phs), the Centers for Disease Control and Prevention (www.cdc.gov), the Centers for Disease Control and Prevention (www.cdc.gov), and the National Center for Infectious Diseases (www.cdc.gov/ncidod). National Health and Safety Performance Standards guidelines for out-of-home child-care programs are available at nrc.uchse.edu/national.

In spaces that are shared by weekday and church groups, wheeled toy shelves that can be turned to the wall and hinged shelves that can be closed are essential. Many toys can be shared, but each group will have toys and supplies that they do not want the other group to use, so these need to be kept out of view. Appropriate storage will simplify what's what and enhance relations between the user groups.

Rooms for Elementary-Aged Children

Elementary-aged children are independent compared to preschoolers. They often arrive at their rooms on their own. Once there, they work around tables in small groups, gather as groups for skits, videos, singing, and stories, and work on long-term projects such as maps, murals, and table-top displays. For these activities they need large, airy, open rooms that are easily cleaned. Kindergartners still need a carpeted area on which to gather for stories. Older children will prefer to bring their chairs to an open area for large group activities.

As elementary-aged children pursue learning activities, they need tables and chairs of the correct height, open bookshelves for Bibles, curriculum resources, and reference books; and a closed cabinet for paper, pencils, and art supplies. Smaller tables (about 30 x 48 inches) are more versatile than the larger "fellowship hall" tables. Four to six children can work independently or cooperatively while seated around one smaller table. Several smaller tables can be pushed together in a variety of configurations for larger group activities. Many classes enjoy trapezoidal tables that can be grouped in interesting ways that give a less school-like feeling.

Hall bathrooms equipped with standard-sized fixtures suit these children fine—but they must be fairly close by. Water fountains are needed in the hall. In-room sinks are appreciated but are not as necessary as in preschool rooms. Elementary classes do need water nearby for cleaning up after projects. A deep sink in a nearby bathroom or a utility sink in a hall closet will work fine.

Playgrounds

Children love playgrounds. A church with a playground says, "Children are welcome!" but many children are hurt, some quite seriously, in playground accidents. When planning outdoor play space for children, careful consideration must be given to both the children's safety and the church's insurance vulnerability.

Because most accidents are related to falls, equipment needs to be selected that includes protective railings and walls that small children cannot slip through or get hung up in. A family yard playset, although likely to be donated, is probably not acceptable. Many schools now prohibit swings. Ongoing attention also needs to be paid to soft ground cover under and around all playground equipment. Most states require 8–12 inches of mulch, pea gravel, or other acceptable ground cover in the "fall area" of all playground equipment. Since this material must be replenished every year, easy access is essential. It is wise to check the National Association for the Education of Young Children's guidelines and state requirements for school playgrounds when planning a playground.

Locating a playground requires careful thought. A playground needs to be easily accessible to children's classrooms. A completely hidden playground sends the message that children are to be hidden away there, but a too visible playground may be considered an attractive nuisance and the church may find itself liable for injuries to unsupervised neighborhood children. A fenced playground is a good solution to keep unsupervised children out and to keep supervised children in. It can also serve as a holding area to which children's groups are evacuated in an emergency.

Working with What Is Less Than Ideal

Thus far I have described the ideal. Few of us live with the ideal. It is even difficult to achieve the ideal when designing a new building with unlimited funds. There are times when children must meet in a space that was clearly not designed as children's space. In these situations, creativity and flexibility are essential, and below are some parameters that will help keep "creative spaces" safe and serviceable.

- Every room needs free egress. It should open either to the outside of the building or to a hallway, not through a room in which another group is meeting.
- Clear plans accepted by all parties are essential. For example, if the children are meeting in the sanctuary before the service, it must be clear when they need to leave and who will move what furnishings where, and this must happen regularly.
- Children's use of the space must not be secondary. For example, as it is clear when and how the sanctuary is to be made available for worship, it must be equally clear that the children are not to be interrupted during their time by organists, choirs, or people setting up communion.
- Assign *adults* rather than children the more cramped, less convenient spaces. Adults have the power and money to make needed long-range changes.

Here are some suggestions for creative use of spaces:

The Sanctuary. The sanctuary most easily accommodates adult classes, but it does offer corners that can welcome groups of children. The front of the sanctuary can also become an elementary classroom. In many cases, tables can be set in front of the first pew and chairs added to the other side of the tables. Easels can be brought in for display space and plastic bins that will slide under the pew can serve as storage for supplies. If there are steps to the chancel, children can sit on them for stories and use them as tables for pencil and paper activities. Add a rocking chair, some carpet, and a crib to space at the back of the sanctuary to create a nursery. Shallow shelves can even be added to the back wall for toys and diapering supplies.

The Fellowship Hall. The fellowship hall or other big rooms can be divided to house several groups. The key to success is to realize that there are no truly soundproof room dividers. Therefore, it is best to place several adult classes or several children's classes in a divided room, but never a mix of adult and children's classes. Spaces should be set up with the teachers' backs to the dividers.

Kitchens. A kitchen with good central floor space can make a great space for older elementary children. With stools instead of chairs, they can work at counters. Water is accessible for ease of cleanup, and cabinets are available for permanent storage space.

Large Closets. Even well-appointed closets can be renovated into unique gathering places for small classes. One small church that I know of houses its three preschoolers in what used to be a closet. The space happens to include part of a stained glass window that bathes the little hideaway with gold light.

Because children go all over the church—into the sanctuary for worship, into fellowship halls for congregational meals, and wherever else the congregation works, plays, and worships—it is important to look at each space from the perspective of children and of parents. Kneeling down in each space to get a child's-eye view will point out simple things that make a big difference to children. Booster seats in pews raise preschoolers so they can see and hear what is going on in worship. Role-playing a visit to church as a parent with young children can highlight special needs. For example, bathrooms near the sanctuary need changing stations and high chairs for infants, along with safe child-sized tables and chairs for youngsters are essential in dining areas. One way members of the property and maintenance committee can keep the promises made to children at baptism or dedication is to provide them with safe, inviting spaces in which to participate in the life of the community. These efforts, although not always easy, will have lasting benefits.

About the Contributors

Cassandra D. Carkuff Williams, Ed.D., an ordained minister, works as a freelance writer, editor, and educational consultant to churches. She has over twenty years experience working with children and currently enjoys serving on the Christian education committee at Calvary Baptist Church, Hermitage, Pennsylvania, where her husband, Chester, is pastor.

Freda Gardner is an elder in the Presbyterian Church (U.S.A.) and a certified Christian educator. She is the Thomas W. Synott Professor Emerita of Christian Education at Princeton Theological Seminary, where she was Director of the School of Christian Education. In 1999 she served as Moderator of the 211th General Assembly of the Presbyterian Church (U.S.A.). She coauthored *Living Alone* with Herbert Anderson, and authored *Active Parenting in the Faith Community: A Biblical and Theological Guide*. She is a member of Nassau Presbyterian Church in Princeton, New Jersey.

Ross A. Thompson, Ph.D., is Carl A. Happold Distinguished Professor of Psychology at the University of Nebraska, where he teaches courses in developmental psychology and studies the emotional growth of young children.

Janet E. Thompson is a teacher at First Plymouth Preschool, an early childhood education program certified by the National Association for the Education of Young Children (NAEYC). Janet and Ross Thompson are members of Westminster Presbyterian Church in Lincoln, Nebraska, where they have served on session and have been active in the church school program. They have conducted teacher in-service seminars and have taught classes for children.

Kathy L. Dawson received a Ph.D. in practical theology in 2001 from Princeton Theological Seminary. She is an instructor in Christian education at Union-PSCE in Richmond, Virginia. A former elementary school teacher, Dr. Dawson is a certified Christian educator and an ordained Presbyterian minister who has published books for children on grief. She has served in the education ministry of congregations in California, Georgia, Alabama, and Massachusetts.

Joyce MacKichan Walker has been the Director of Christian Education at Nassau Presbyterian Church in Princeton, New Jersey, since 1988. She is a 1979 graduate of the Presbyterian School of Christian Education (now Union-PSCE) and has been a Certified Christian Educator since 1983. She has served on the Certification

Council, the national cabinet of the Association of Presbyterian Church Educators, a General Assembly work group on the role and status of Christian educators. and a task force on Educational Design for Ordination of Christian Educators. She is a member of the leadership team for returning class events for graduates of Princeton Theological Seminary, serves as a workshop leader at APCE and in other settings, and occasionally is a Visiting Lecturer at Princeton Theological Seminary.

Rebecca L. Davis is a Minister of Word and Sacrament and Certified Educator in the Presbyterian Church (U.S.A.). She served the church as a Director of Christian Education and Early Childhood Development Center, an associate pastor and a pastor, an associate general presbyter, and most recently as the Coordinator of the Religious Action Division for the Children's Defense Fund. She was the organizing moderator of the Presbyterian Child Advocacy Network, a member of the Year of the Child Planning Team, and a Children's Ministry Consultant. She is currently a doctoral student at Union-PSCE in Richmond, Virginia.

Carol A. Wehrheim has written and edited materials in the following curricula series: *Living the Word, Doing the Word, Bible Discovery, The Storyteller Series, Discipleship Alive! The Inviting Word, Celebrate*, and *Covenant People*. She is also an editor for *Bible Quest* (adult) and *Seasons of the Spirit* (ages 9–11). She has written *So Great a Cloud of Witnesses: A Survey of Church History* for the *We Believe* curriculum and is on the sixth grade teaching team at Nassau Presbyterian Church, Princeton, New Jersey, where she is a member.

Patricia Griggs has been teaching in church school since she was thirteen years old. For over thirty years, she and her husband, Don, managed Griggs Educational Services. For the first fifteen years of her career, she served as Director of Editorial Services and Director of Publications and Promotion, writing resources, working as co-editor for the *Faith for Life* curriculum materials, and providing leadership training for LOGOS System Associates. In 1993 Pat and Don were honored as Educators of the Year by the Association of Presbyterian Church Educators. Although retired, she continues her involvement in Christian education.

Mary Anne Fowlkes, Ph.D., is Professor Emerita of Childhood Education, Union-PSCE. She recently retired to Santa Fe after teaching in the area of children's ministries from 1987 to 2001. She was formerly a director of Christian education, a kindergarten teacher, and director of a church's weekday kindergarten. She is the author of *The Church Cares for Children*, and from 1980 until 1987 she served as a consultant on weekday programs for churches. She taught early childhood education at the University of Louisville where she served on the board of Community Coordinated Child Care and as a consultant to Jefferson County Public Schools.

Jean Floyd Love, Ed.D., is a former director of Christian Education, specializing in children's ministry. She was named Educator of the Year in 1996 by the Association of Presbyterian Church Educators. She is coauthor of Get Ready, Get Set, Worship. She has taught continuing education courses at Presbyterian School of Christian Education, Austin Seminary, and Columbia Seminary and has led workshops in children's ministry at Montreat Conference Center in North Carolina.

Sara Covin Juengst, D. D., is a retired Presbyterian minister and certified Christian educator who was a missionary to the Congo for eleven years. She also served as the Staff Associate for Mutual Mission in the Presbyterian Church (U.S.A.) and as Director of Continuing Education at Columbia Theology Seminary. She is the author of numerous articles, curriculum materials, and eight books, including *Sharing Faith with Children* and *The Road Home: Images for the Spiritual Journey*. She lives in Willington, South Carolina, with her husband, Dan, a retired anthropology professor.

Elaine Barnett is a certified Christian educator and elder. She served congregations in North Carolina and is currently serving as Associate Executive Presbyter for Nurture for the Presbytery of Tampa Bay. She is coauthor of *The Big Book of Presbyterian Stewardship* published by Geneva Press in 2000, *A Companion Leaders' Guide for Healthy Congregations* published by Spartan Publications in 2000, and *Leader's Guide for AVENUES to United Decision Making*, a 1998 publication of Del Poling Resources. She lives in Bradenton, Florida, with her husband, Jim, a development officer for the Presbyterian Foundation.

Carolyn Brown has served in churches in Connecticut, North Carolina, Tennessee, and Virginia and is currently the Director of Children's Ministries at Trinity Presbyterian Church in Atlanta, Georgia. She is the author of several books published by Abingdon Press, including *You Can Preach to the Kids, Too!*, *Developing Christian Education in the Smaller Church*, and *Gateways to Worship*.